insight text guide

Fabrice Wilmann

The Hunger Games

Suzanne Collins

First published in 2023, reprinted in 2024, 2025, 2026.

Insight Publications Pty Ltd
3/350 Charman Road
Cheltenham VIC 3192
Australia
Tel: +61 3 8571 4950
Email: books@insightpublications.com.au

www.insightpublications.com.au

A catalogue record for this book is available from the National Library of Australia

Suzanne Collins' The Hunger Games / Fabrice Wilmann

Fabrice Wilmann asserts the moral right to be identified as the author of this work.

ISBNs:
9781922771872 (print)
9781922771889 (digital)

Cover design by Hayley Sinnatt

Proudly Printed in Australia by Ligare Book Printers

contents

CHARACTER MAP

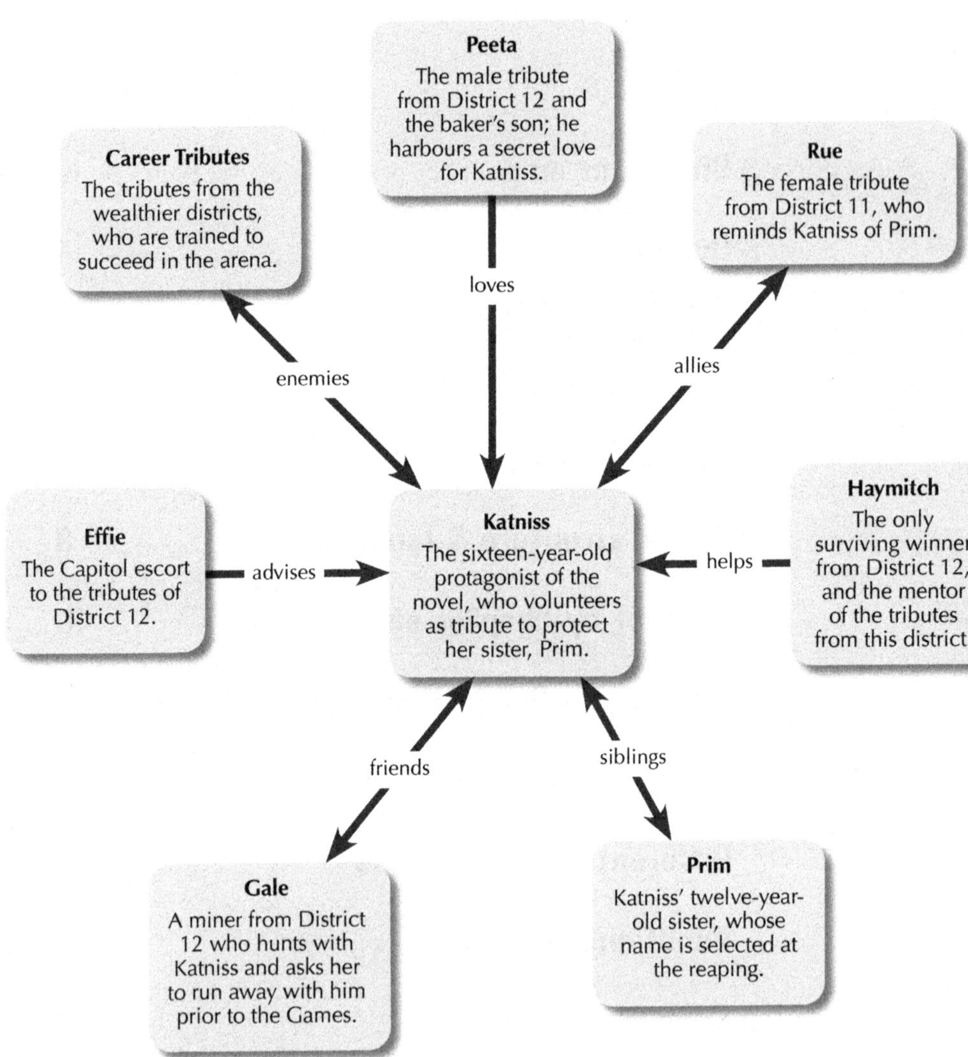

OVERVIEW

About the author

Suzanne Collins is an American author and television writer who was born in Hartford, Connecticut in 1962. Throughout her childhood she and her family moved around often as her father was an officer in the US Air Force. She has a BA in theatre and telecommunications from Indiana University, as well as a Master of Fine Arts in dramatic writing from the New York University Tisch School of the Arts.

In 1991 Collins began her career as a staff writer for Nickelodeon, contributing to several children's television shows including *Little Bear* and the Emmy-nominated *Clarissa Explains It All*. After meeting a children's author while working on the Kids' WB show *Generation O!*, Collins was inspired to write her own children's book. Her first novel, *Gregor the Overlander*, was published in 2003, the first in a five-book fantasy/war series titled *The Underland Chronicles*.

The first book in the *Hunger Games* trilogy was published in 2008. It became a *New York Times* bestseller and has been sold into fifty-four territories and translated into fifty-two languages. The other two books in the original trilogy are *Catching Fire* (2009) and *Mockingjay* (2010). A prequel, *The Ballad of Songbirds and Snakes*, was released in 2020.

A film adaptation of *The Hunger Games* starring Oscar-winner Jennifer Lawrence was released in 2012, with Collins working as a scriptwriter alongside the film's director Gary Ross and screenwriter Billy Ray. It was followed by *The Hunger Games: Catching Fire* (2013), *The Hunger Games: Mockingjay Part 1* (2014) and *The Hunger Games: Mockingjay Part 2* (2015).

In 2010 Collins was named one of *Time* magazine's most influential people, and in 2016 she was presented with the Author's Guild Award for Distinguished Service to the Literary Community.

Synopsis

The novel is set in a fictional nation called Panem, run by a despotic government that rules the surrounding twelve districts from the comfort of the Capitol. Each year it hosts the Hunger Games – a warning to anyone who dares to rebel against its authority – in which two children or tributes from each of the twelve districts must fight to the death, with only one surviving.

Katniss Everdeen, the protagonist of the story, volunteers as tribute from District 12 when her younger sister, Prim, is randomly selected in a process called the reaping. She and Peeta, their district's male tribute, are taken to the Capitol, where they are mentored by Haymitch, a previous winner of the Games from District 12, and their Capitol escort, Effie Trinket.

The Games begin. In the arena, Katniss escapes the pandemonium at the Cornucopia and flees into the woods, while Peeta appears to team up with the Career Tributes. The Gamemakers start a fire to drive the tributes together, during which Katniss is injured by a hurling fireball. She is forced to scale a tree to avoid the Career Tributes and the following morning drops a tracker-jacker nest on them, killing two tributes. She is stung herself in the process and begins to hallucinate; Peeta helps her to evade Cato, one of the Career Tributes, showing that he has not betrayed her. Katniss forms an alliance with Rue, the girl tribute from District 11, and together they are able to destroy the Careers' supplies at the Cornucopia. Rue is killed by the boy from District 1, whom Katniss murders in an act of vengeance.

The voice of Games announcer Claudius Templesmith booms into the arena, declaring a change of rules: there can be two winners if they hail from the same district. Katniss finds Peeta, who is badly wounded after his altercation with Cato, and tries to nurse him back to health, though he needs proper medicine. When Claudius announces a 'feast' at the Cornucopia where the supplies needed by each contestant will be available, Katniss goes against Peeta's wishes. She is attacked by

Clove and saved by Thresh, who kills Clove for her part in Rue's death, and who then lets Katniss escape because of her loyalty to Rue. Katniss gives Peeta the medicine and he recovers; he then takes care of her in her injured state. Peeta accidentally outfoxes Foxface, who consumes poisonous nightlock berries and dies.

Peeta, Katniss and Cato – the three remaining tributes after Cato kills Thresh – are driven to the lake by the Gamemakers, who unleash 'muttations' to attack them. Katniss manages to shoot an arrow at Cato while he has Peeta in his grasp; he falls from the Cornucopia and is savaged before Katniss finally puts him out of his misery. Claudius announces that the rules have reverted and that only one winner will be declared. In a calculated act of rebellion, Katniss and Peeta both prepare to eat the nightlock, thereby ensuring there will be no winner at all. In response, Claudius quickly announces that they are both the winners of the Games.

Katniss and Peeta are taken aboard a hovercraft, where doctors operate on Peeta, giving him a prosthetic leg. Back in the Capitol, Haymitch warns Katniss she is still in danger for her act of rebellion. During the winner's interview with Caesar, Katniss successfully passes off the act of rebellion as an act of intense love.

Character summaries

Katniss Everdeen

Katniss is the sixteen-year-old protagonist of the book, who volunteers herself as tribute from District 12 to save her sister from participating in the deadly Hunger Games.

Peeta Mellark

Peeta is the male tribute from District 12, who has feelings for Katniss.

Gale Hawthorne

Gale is Katniss' closest friend in District 12, with whom she goes hunting.

Haymitch Abernathy

One of only two winning tributes from District 12 (and the only one still alive), Haymitch is always drunk and is viewed as an embarrassment by the people of his district.

President Snow

Snow is the president of Panem, who maintains control over the nation through force and oppression.

Effie Trinket

The official escort and mentor to the tributes of District 12, Effie is described as 'maniacally upbeat' (p.9) and having a 'scary white grin, pinkish hair and spring green suit' (p.21).

Cinna

Cinna is Katniss' lead stylist and costumer, who also becomes her friend.

Caesar Flickerman

Caesar conducts interviews with the tributes, usually in front of a live audience each year; the interviews are also broadcast on television.

Rue

Rue is the female tribute from District 11, with whom Katniss forges an alliance, and who dies in Katniss' arms in the arena.

Primrose (Prim) Everdeen

Prim is Katniss' younger sister, whose name is drawn during the reaping in District 12.

BACKGROUND & CONTEXT

Collins drew inspiration for *The Hunger Games* from a number of sources, both contemporary and classical, as well as from her own life experiences.

The Vietnam and Iraq Wars

War is a common theme explored in Collins' works, likely a result of growing up with a father who was in the US Air Force. He fought in the Vietnam War and experienced firsthand the horror of wartime and the disastrous effects of poverty and starvation. Collins reflects these ideas in her book, which is set in a fictional nation where the districts lost a war against the Capitol; its citizens were thereby forced to live in poor conditions and suffer under a brutal regime.

The Iraq War (2003–2011), which was taking place while Collins was writing the book, was another inspiration. Footage of the destruction of the land and the suffering of citizens and soldiers was played constantly on US television, meaning people became accustomed to such displays of violence and ultimately desensitising them to it. According to Collins, the idea for *The Hunger Games,* which blends war with reality television, came as she 'was flipping through the channels one night between reality television programs and actual footage of the Iraq War' (Collins, *The New York Times* 2018). This idea is particularly relevant for the readership of Collins' book – 'a generation who grew up through 9/11, the Madrid bombings, the London bombings and Islamic State terrors. They see danger piped down their smartphones and beheadings on their Facebook page' (Hughes 2015).

Reality television

At its core, the Hunger Games is a reality-television competition, one in which every moment of the fighting and the emotional responses of competitors is captured on cameras and beamed to a national audience. This recalls a number of contemporary US reality television shows, such as *Survivor* and *American Idol*.

There are several features of competitive reality television that can be seen throughout the book. These include the progressive elimination of competitors (though in *The Hunger Games* this occurs through the deaths of the tributes), the styling of participants in order to make the show more entertaining (as shown in the makeovers of the tributes prior to the opening ceremony), and the intervention of the producers to heighten the drama (evidenced in the Gamemakers changing the rules halfway through the Games). Just like in real life, viewers in the Capitol dissect and analyse the actions of the competitors – 'But what a good time Claudius Templesmith must be having with his guest commentators, dissecting Peeta's behaviour, my reaction' (p.200) – and betting on who will win: 'The betting must be getting really hot in the Capitol. They'll be doing special features on each of us now. Probably interviewing our friends and families' (p.273).

Collins is scathing in her depiction of audiences of reality television, who show little or no compassion or empathy for the real-life people broadcast on their screens. The Capitol audience is shown to be callously uncaring about the plight of the tributes, who are teenagers reaped from impoverished districts, forced to participate in blood sport for the entertainment of their wealthy oppressors. Even those who mean well, like Katniss' stylist team, exhibit the same disconnected, voyeuristic qualities seen in viewers of shows such as *The Kardashians* or *Love Island*. Despite watching someone they know undergo a prolonged traumatic experience, they are still concerned first and foremost with themselves: 'it's all about where they were or what they were doing or how they felt when a specific event occurred' (p.429).

Theseus and the Minotaur

Collins' main classical source of inspiration is the Greek myth of Theseus and the Minotaur, in which, as a punishment for past crimes, Minos forces Athens to sacrifice seven youths and seven maidens to the Minotaur, which kills them in a vast labyrinth. Angered by this brutal practice, one year Theseus volunteers to be a tribute. He travels to Crete where Minos' daughter Ariadne helps him to find his way through the labyrinth and kill the Minotaur. In doing so, he saves Athens from the terrible sacrifice of its youth and becomes the king and unifier of the nation. Collins explains, 'I was such a huge Greek mythology geek as a kid, it's impossible for it not to come into play in my storytelling. The connection to the myth of Theseus happened immediately' (*The New York Times* 2018).

As in the legend of Theseus, the twelve districts of Panem in *The Hunger Games* are required to send young male and female tributes to certain death. And like Theseus, who volunteers to be a tribute in order to kill the Minotaur, Katniss volunteers to be a tribute in order to save her younger sister, Prim.

GENRE, STRUCTURE & LANGUAGE

Genre

It would be appropriate to refer to *The Hunger Games* as a dystopian novel. It is set in a fictional nightmarish future in which a despotic government controls its citizens, who are forced to live in districts that produce commodities such as food and coal for use in the Capitol. Those who live in the districts are kept in line by threat of violence and subjugation, exemplified on a national scale and broadcast live around the country in the form of the annual Hunger Games, in which each year twenty-four children from the districts are forced to fight to the death.

The Hunger Games could also be considered a young-adult novel or bildungsroman (coming-of-age story). Like other novels in this space, *The Hunger Games* is told from the perspective of its teenage protagonist, Katniss Everdeen, who must navigate issues surrounding her identity and romantic relationships while trying to stay alive.

Structure

The novel is divided into three parts ('The Tributes', 'The Games' and 'The Victor') and twenty-seven chapters. Told from Katniss' point of view, the story is narrated chronologically, beginning with the reaping and ending with the conclusion of this particular year's Hunger Games.

There are short flashbacks or recounts of memories interspersed throughout, as Katniss reflects on her past – for example, the death of her father; Peeta saving her family from starvation by giving her bread; and Katniss learning to hunt and developing a partnership with Gale.

Language

Collins uses a clear and direct writing style, making it easy for readers to follow the plot and understand the characters' motivations. The language is not overly complex, making it accessible to a wide range of readers. It is often fast-paced, particularly during the Games themselves, with Collins using action verbs and short, impactful sentences to build tension and keep readers engaged – for example, 'It's that quick. The death of the boy from District 3' (p.271).

The story is narrated in the first person, allowing readers to gain insight into Katniss' thoughts, emotions and experiences. The tone is often conversational, helping to create a strong connection between the reader and the protagonist.

CHAPTER-BY-CHAPTER ANALYSIS

PART I – The Tributes

Chapter 1 (pp.3–24)

Summary: *Katniss and Gale go hunting in the woods, then to the black market to trade their quarry; the reaping is held in the town square; Katniss' sister Primrose is randomly selected as the female tribute from District 12.*

Chapter 1 introduces the reader to the protagonist, Katniss Everdeen, a pragmatic, headstrong sixteen-year-old who is both the breadwinner for and protector of her family. She is deeply critical of her mother for failing to be present after the death of Katniss' father – 'I try to forgive her for my father's sake. But to be honest, I'm not the forgiving type' (p.10) – but a softer side of her is shown in how she cares deeply for her younger sister, Primrose, who she describes as 'the only person in the world I'm certain I love' (p.11).

Presented through the first-person perspective of Katniss, the opening chapter also helps to set up the world of the novel and explain the history of the dystopian future in which it is set. The story takes place in Panem, 'the country that rose up out of the ashes of a place that was once called North America' (p.21). The Hunger Games is the tool used by the ruling Capitol government to control the districts. This event, on which the plot of the novel focuses, pits twenty-four tributes – one girl and one boy from each of the twelve districts – in a battle royale fight-to-the-death, where only one tribute remains standing. It is both horrific and inhumane, and alludes to the oppression and violence that haunts Katniss and other innocent bystanders like her.

Katniss lives in District 12, the farthest district from the Capitol and one of the poorest. The people from this district are tasked with mining coal for the Capitol. The area of District 12 in which Katniss lives is nicknamed the Seam, as it is at the edge of town, separated from the surrounding woods by an electrified 'high chain-link fence topped with barbed-wire loops' (p.5) that Katniss often bypasses to go hunting.

The chapter ends on the climactic revelation that it is Katniss' sister Primrose who has been chosen as the female tribute from District 12.

Key point

The idea of trauma is developed early in the book, specifically Katniss' trauma from losing her father at a young age: 'he was blown to bits in a mine explosion ... I was eleven then. Five years later, I still wake up screaming for him to run' (p.6). While this trauma plays out in her nightmares, it does not prevent Katniss from doing what must be done to keep her and her family alive. Her mother is unable to do the same; she is made 'blank and unreachable' (p.10) as her daughters suffer from a lack of functional parental figures in their lives, causing a seemingly irreparable rift between her and Katniss.

Q What are your first impressions of Katniss?

Q How does Collins develop her fictional world and portray it clearly to her readers?

Chapter 2 (pp.25–40)

Summary: *Katniss immediately volunteers as tribute to save her sister from certain death in the arena; Peeta Mellark is selected as the male tribute from District 12; Katniss reflects on an earlier encounter with Peeta.*

Volunteering as a tribute is viewed very differently among the different districts. Whereas people in Districts 1, 2 and 4 fight over the chance for glory by participating in the Games, 'volunteers are all but extinct' in District 12, 'where the word *tribute* is pretty much synonymous with the word *corpse*' (p.27). Katniss' sacrificial act is 'the radical thing' (p.31) and highlights her devotion to her family.

Key point

The first signs of rebellion, a key theme of the series, are explored at the beginning of this chapter. After Katniss has volunteered as tribute, her fellow townspeople touch the middle three fingers of their left hand to their lips and hold them out to her, 'an old and rarely used gesture of our district ... it means thanks, it means admiration, it means goodbye to someone you love' (p.29). Though it is a relatively minor gesture, it shows that the citizens of Panem have not been completely suppressed by the Capitol.

This chapter introduces the idea of facades and keeping up appearances. Knowing that the Games are just as much about how a person presents themselves as survival and combat skills, Katniss fights away her tears and attempts to present a stoic front: 'When they televise the replay of the reapings tonight, everyone will make note of my tears, and I'll be marked as an easy target. A weakling. I will give no one that satisfaction' (pp.27–8).

Peeta Mellark is chosen as the male tribute for District 12. The first thing that Katniss notices about him in this moment are his blue eyes showing 'the alarm I've seen so often in prey' (p.31) – this ties in with the motif of hunting and survival, as the tributes will all be prey once they enter the arena. Despite Katniss trying 'to convince [herself] it doesn't matter' that she and Peeta 'are not friends' (p.31), she recalls an earlier interaction between the two that was life-changing for her and allowed her to overcome one of her darkest moments: 'To this day, I can never shake the connection between this boy, Peeta Mellark, and the bread that gave me hope' (p.39).

Q How would you describe the relationship between Katniss and Peeta at this stage of the novel?

Chapter 3 (pp.41–57)

Summary: *Katniss and Peeta say goodbye to their loved ones; Katniss receives the mockingjay pin; Katniss and Peeta take the train to the Capitol.*

Rather than being drawn into an emotional response that she knows can overwhelm her and negatively affect her preparations for the games, Katniss focuses on pragmatic matters when saying goodbye to her family. She tells them 'all the things they must remember to do, now that [she] will not be there to do them for them' (p.42).

Key point

One of the most prominent motifs of the novel, which also appears on the cover of the book, are mockingjays. These birds are the result of the breeding of mockingbirds with Capitol-bred 'muttations' known as jabberjays, which had 'the ability to memorize and repeat whole human conversations' (p.52). These birds act as symbols of rebellion, 'something of a slap in the face to the Capitol' (p.51). Additionally, they carry sentimental meaning for Katniss, reminding her of her father, who 'was particularly fond of mockingjays' and their ability to 'recreate songs' (p.52).

Q How important is it for Katniss to wipe her face 'clean of emotions' (p.49)? What are the repercussions if she shows too much emotion?

Chapter 4 (pp.58–73)

Summary: *Katniss reflects on her home and her family; Peeta and Katniss have a brief altercation with Haymitch, showing him their potential in the arena, which leads him to offer them his help; they reach the Capitol.*

Despite Haymitch's poor reputation – as Katniss notes, 'the rich people who back tributes ... expect someone classier than Haymitch to deal with' (p.68) – he shows in this chapter that he can help Katniss and Peeta in the arena. The only reason he chooses to do so, however, is because, unlike past tributes from this district, they show promise; after Peeta lunges at him and Katniss drives a knife in between his hand and a bottle of spirits, he responds with, 'Did I actually get a pair of fighters this year?' (p.69). This reinforces the idea that the tributes from District 12 are generally considered dead before even entering the arena, and not worth the time or trouble of being trained.

Key point

Appearances are very important to the citizens of the Capitol, and a recurring motif of the book. The tributes must present themselves as strong in order to intimidate their competitors as well as to help them gain sponsors from the wealthy elite of the Capitol. But while 'the Hunger Games aren't a beauty contest', Katniss points out that 'the best-looking tributes always seem to pull more sponsors' (p.70). This reflects modern society and the idea of pretty privilege, an idea that Collins appears to be criticising.

Q In what ways is a kind Peeta Mellark 'far more dangerous to [Katniss] than an unkind one' (p.59)?

Q What does this chapter reveal about Katniss' sensitive side?

Chapter 5 (pp.74–88)

Summary: *Katniss is prepped by her team of stylists, led by Cinna; she and Peeta ride in the opening ceremony; President Snow gives the official welcome.*

This is our first introduction to Capitol-dwelling citizens other than Effie. The members of Katniss' prep team, comprising Venia, Octavia and Flavius, are described by Katniss as 'total idiots' (p.76), reflecting how people like them are generally viewed by citizens outside of the Capitol. However, Katniss also notes that 'they're sincerely trying to help me' (p.76), suggesting that not everyone who lives in the Capitol is terrible and that, just like any other group in society, its citizens are nuanced.

The lead stylist, Cinna, is depicted as a normal, stoic figure, even if one of Katniss' initial impressions is that his 'calm and normal demeanour masks a complete madman.' (p.82). His creativity and flair suggest that individuality has not been completely lost in the superficiality of the Capitol. He and his co-stylist, Portia, who 'see it as [their] job to make the District Twelve tributes unforgettable' (p.81), show genuine care for Katniss, helping her to feel comfortable in her new surroundings.

'Leaving a trail of fire off the flowing capes' (p.85), Katniss and Peeta are the standout performers in the opening ceremony. This is aided by the act they put on for the crowd, with Katniss blowing them kisses and the pair holding hands. As a result of their strong showing, Katniss feels a 'flicker of hope' rising up in her for the first time: 'Surely there must be one sponsor willing to take me on! And with a little extra help, some food, the right weapon, why should I count myself out of the Games?' (p.86).

Q How does this chapter reinforce the importance of appearances?

Chapter 6 (pp.89–104)

Summary: *Katniss and Peeta are taken to the Training Centre, their home until they enter the arena; Katniss recalls the story of the Avox or 'traitor'.*

Effie shares that she is advertising Katniss and Peeta to 'everyone who's anyone in the Capitol' (p.90). While this is a nice gesture on the surface, it's clear that she is doing it to further her career; furthermore, she calls District 12 barbaric, which Katniss notes is 'ironic coming from a woman helping to prepare us for slaughter' (p.90).

This chapter introduces the concept of an Avox, 'someone who committed a crime' (p.94) against the Capitol. As soon as Katniss recognises the girl serving them, she knows 'some bad memory is associated with her' (p.94). She goes on to recall the story of how she and Gale failed to help the girl, before the boy she was with was murdered and she was taken in one of the government's hovercrafts. Although she 'wondered if [they] could have helped them escape' (p.98), Katniss' actions, or inaction, reflect the very human ideas of self-preservation and survival, which will come to the fore in the arena. Having been distracted by the glitz and glamour of the Capitol, Katniss is frightened by 'the girl with her maimed tongue', who reminds her that she's not here 'to model flashy costumes and eat delicacies' but 'to die a bloody death while the crowds urge on [her] killer' (p.100).

Q How do Effie's views of District 12 reflect the wider view of the districts by Capitol dwellers?

Q What is the significance of the story of the Avox?

Chapter 7 (pp.105–24)

Summary: *Haymitch gives Katniss and Peeta advice before they commence their training; the private sessions with the Gamemakers take place.*

Preparing for the group training that all the tributes will participate in, Katniss dresses in her usual attire, noting that 'this is the first time since the morning of the reaping that I resemble myself. No fancy hair and clothes, no flaming capes. Just me' (p.106). Coming back to who she knows she is – the antithesis of the artificial, insincere world of the Capitol – helps to ground Katniss.

Haymitch gives the two of them sound advice for their training sessions, telling Katniss to hide her archery skills until her private session with the Gamemakers, and Peeta not to 'reveal how much [he] can lift in front of the other tributes' (p.112). He also tells them to learn a new skill at group training. Though they keep to their word and hide their greatest strengths, 'Peeta excels in hand-to-hand combat, and [Katniss] sweep[s] the edible plants test without blinking an eye' (p.118). In addition, they learn 'a simple, excellent trap that will leave a human competitor dangling by a leg from a tree' (p.116), a skill that will come in handy when they are in the arena.

In her private session with the Gamemakers, Katniss becomes 'furious' with them for not having the 'decency to pay attention to [her]' while her life is on the line (p.124). Displaying a sense of rebellion that she is becoming more and more known for, she shoots an arrow towards the Gamemakers, who watch, startled, as it pierces the apple in the mouth of the roast pig and pins the apple against the wall.

Q What are your first impressions of the Career Tributes? What do they reveal about the differences between their districts and those further away from the Capitol?

Chapter 8 (pp.125–37)

Summary: *The training scores are released and Katniss receives the top mark from the Gamemakers; she reflects on her relationship with Gale.*

Katniss cries after her act of rebellion against the Gamemakers, thinking she has ruined everything. She is self-aware, recognising that she wasn't thinking but was simply acting out of anger, but also selfless, caring less about what happens to her than to her family: 'Who cares what they do to me? What really scares me is what they might do to my mother and Prim; how my family might suffer now because of my impulsiveness' (p.126). For Katniss, everything ultimately comes back to her love for her family and her desire to protect them.

Her team, including Haymitch and Effie, makes her realise that what she did wasn't so terrible, as the Gamemakers can't reprimand her without revealing what occurred in the private session: 'And I realize the impossible has happened. They have actually cheered me up' (p.130). Even Effie, who has so far shown greater loyalty to the Capitol than to her charges, acknowledges that 'just because you come from District Twelve is no excuse to ignore you' (p.130).

Q Why do you think Katniss reflects on her relationship with Gale at this point in the novel? What are the similarities and differences between their relationship and the one between Katniss and Peeta?

Chapter 9 (pp.138–58)

Summary: *Effie and Haymitch coach Katniss and Peeta separately before their interviews; the tributes are interviewed by Caesar.*

The previous chapter ends with the revelation that 'Peeta has asked to be coached separately' (p.137), which elicits feelings of anger and betrayal in Katniss. During their prep session, Effie instructs Katniss to smile more, to put on a mask the way that she sometimes does: 'I'm smiling at you even though you're aggravating me' (p.140). This is another example of the superficial facade representative of the Capitol.

Haymitch ponders how Katniss should present herself to the audience in her interview. He details her positive attributes first – volunteering to save her sister, her unforgettable costume designed by Cinna, her top training score – before stating that, while people are intrigued, 'no one knows who [she is]' (p.141). He criticises her personality, telling her that she needs to come across as more warm and friendly, otherwise the audience won't want to sponsor her. Cinna is the one to encourage her, reminding her that she impresses people and draws them to her when she is just being herself: 'The prep team adores you. You even won over the Gamemakers ... No one can help but admire your spirit' (p.147).

The interviews are conducted by 'Caesar Flickerman, the man who has hosted the interviews for more than forty years ... It's a little scary because his appearance has been virtually unchanged during all that time' (p.150). Here, Collins seems to be critiquing the modern-day culture of face augmentation, Botox and cosmetic surgery. Caesar 'really does his best to make the tributes shine' (p.151), reinforcing the idea that not everyone in the Capitol is inherently evil. He helps to make Katniss feel at ease, allowing her to show the softer and more humorous side of her personality, eliciting from the crowd laughter at her self-deprecating comments and empathy as she talks about Prim.

Q How does this chapter provide a critique of reality television?

Q How does Collins create tension at the ends of chapters and parts?

PART II – The Games

Chapter 10 (pp.161–78)

Summary: *Katniss attacks Peeta for declaring his love for her onstage; they argue the night before the Games begin; Cinna returns to Katniss her mockingjay pin, which she had previously left on a discarded outfit; the tributes are fitted with a tracking device before they enter the arena.*

The cliffhanger of the previous chapter, in which Peeta announces to everyone that he's in love with the girl who 'came here with [him]' (p.158), sets the stage for a confrontation between Katniss and Peeta. While 'Peeta has absolutely wiped the rest of [his competitors] off the map with his declaration of love' (p.162), Katniss is incensed that he has made her look vulnerable and the object of men's affections. His actions show that he is either strategic and manipulative or truthful and sensitive. Whatever the reason, the desired effect is achieved: the audience cares about and is invested in the relationship between 'the star-crossed lovers from District Twelve' (p.164) – a reference to Shakespeare's *Romeo and Juliet*.

Katniss and Peeta say goodbye to Haymitch and Effie, who are tasked with securing them sponsors while they are in the arena. Effie is both sentimental and brash, jumping from tearfully thanking them 'for being the best tributes it has ever been her privilege to sponsor' to hoping to 'finally get promoted to a decent district next year' (pp.167–8). Haymitch is pragmatic, giving them guidance on what to do when the gong sounds: 'clear out, put as much distance as you can between yourselves and the others, and find a source of water' (p.168).

Q How does Katniss cope with the dread before entering the arena?

Q What issues of morality does Peeta raise in this chapter?

Chapter 11 (pp.179–94)

Summary: *The Games begin, as the tributes are released from their landing pads; the Career Tributes head straight for the weapons at the Cornucopia; Katniss escapes a knife being thrown at her and flees to the forest; by the end of the first day it is announced that eleven tributes are dead.*

Katniss is tempted to try to take a bow and quiver of arrows she sees at the Cornucopia, knowing 'that the Career Tributes who survive the bloodbath will divide up most of these life-sustaining spoils' (p.180). She knows she is fast and is seriously contemplating this action when she is distracted by Peeta, which derails her plans and angers her further.

Key point

The first death of the novel is described in graphic language: 'splattering my face with blood', 'the warm, sticky spray' (p.182). After the build-up of the previous part of the novel, the immediate portrayal of violence is jarring and visceral. This is likely intentional, with Collins reminding readers of the pure horror of the situation and the real, gory consequences of forcing children to kill.

Katniss escapes from the bloodbath at the Cornucopia with a backpack, a piece of plastic, some bread and a knife that was thrown at her by one of the other tributes. Following Haymitch's advice, she flees into the woods, trying to put as much distance as possible between her and the Career Tributes. Linking back to the start of the novel, where her fondness for wilderness in District 12 is explored, she similarly finds these woods 'rejuvenating' (p.184).

Q Why do you think Collins chooses to describe the violence in such graphic terms, considering the main audience for her book?

Q What game do you think Peeta is playing? Do you think it will pay off in the long run?

Chapter 12 (pp.195–207)

Summary: *Peeta appears to team up with the Career Tributes and kills a helpless tribute to prove his loyalty to them; Katniss snares a rabbit and finds a source of water.*

Katniss is horrified and infuriated to observe, from her vantage point high in a tree, that Peeta has teamed up 'with the Career wolf pack to hunt the rest of [them] down' (p.196). She explains that he would be poorly received back home for acting so treacherously, as the Career Tributes are hated universally. Katniss overhears one of them asking, 'Why don't we just kill him now and get it over with?' (p.196), revealing that the Careers are just using Peeta, but she also thinks the alliance is genuine on his part, and sees this as a betrayal. The Careers also think that Katniss is 'simple-minded' (p.197) because all they've seen is her playing the part of a compliant girl, 'spinning around in that dress' (p.197) – another example of how appearances can be deceptive.

Katniss knows that her every act is being watched and that she 'need[s] to look one step ahead of the game' (p.198). She shows off her hunting skills by snaring and cooking a rabbit, wanting sponsors to see that she can hunt, 'that [she's] a good bet because [she] won't be lured into traps as easily as the others will by hunger' (p.199). Katniss clearly understands the bigger picture of how the Games operate.

Katniss' logical thinking and deductive skills, even when she is deprived of food and water, are again displayed as she realises that 'there's only one good reason Haymitch could be withholding water from me. Because he knows I've almost found it' (p.204). Thus, she struggles on, and is able to find a source of water.

Q What similarities between the Games and reality television are depicted in this chapter?

Chapter 13 (pp.208–23)

Summary: *A fire blazes through the woods, forcing Katniss to flee; fireballs are flung at her and one damages her leg; the Careers find her but she manages to avoid them by climbing a tree.*

The Gamemakers create a fire to remind the tributes that they are mere pawns, used for the entertainment of others. In contrast to the volatile and harrowing experience of trying to escape the fire, with fireballs and smoke, 'somewhere, in a cool and spotless room, a Gamemaker sits at a set of controls, fingers on the trigger that could end [the tributes' lives] in a second' (p.212). This picture emblemises the social inequality rampant in the world of Panem.

Using her knowledge of the Games – developed from being forced to watch every year, along with all other citizens in the districts – Katniss is able to figure out her next move: 'A lifetime of watching the Hunger Games lets me know that certain areas of the arena are rigged for certain attacks' (p.212).

Though she escapes the immediate danger of the fire, she is led to the Career Tributes and Peeta. While she may be outnumbered, she uses what may have initially been perceived as a disadvantage – her size – to her own benefit by scaling the heights of a tree that the heavier Career Tributes cannot reach. Once a safe distance away, she teases them by conversing normally, knowing that 'the crowd will love it' (p.220).

Q How important are attributes such as resilience in the Games? Do you think they are more important than strategy?

Chapter 14 (pp.224–35)

Summary: *Sitting in a nearby tree, District 11 tribute Rue alerts Katniss to a tracker-jacker nest; Katniss receives medicine via a sponsor; she saws off the tracker-jacker nest, dropping it on the Career Tributes and Peeta; Katniss begins hallucinating from the tracker-jacker stings, but Peeta helps her escape.*

Katniss decides to drop the tracker-jacker nest down onto the Careers and Peeta, and in doing so sets the groundwork for an alliance with Rue. She reasons that 'since she tipped me off, it only seems fair to warn her' (p.229) that she was dropping the nest. Katniss declares that she would rather Rue win because 'even if it means a little extra food for my family, the idea of Peeta being crowned victor is unbearable' (p.229). Her anger, pride and feeling of betrayal overcome her sense of duty to her family, reminding readers of her brash and passionate temperament.

Katniss unleashes the tracker-jacker nest on the Careers, indirectly causing the death of two tributes, the first time she has been responsible for the death of other human beings, though she does not have time to consider the moral and ethical implications of this. In trying to pry the bow and arrows from the dead body of one of the tributes she helped to kill, Katniss begins to hallucinate, an effect of being stung by the tracker jackers while sawing the nest from the tree. She is saved from Cato by Peeta, whose true motives start to become clearer to both Katniss and readers.

Q How important are alliances and relationships in *The Hunger Games*?

Q How have Katniss' natural skills benefited her so far in the arena?

Chapter 15 (pp.236–50)

Summary: *Katniss and Rue form an alliance; they discuss life in their respective districts; Rue reveals that Peeta is no longer with the Careers, and surmises that he had to run from them after he saved Katniss.*

Thinking about Peeta saving her, Katniss questions whether he is 'simply working the Lover Boy angle' or if he is 'actually trying to protect me' (p.238). She is unsure what to make of her fellow District 12 tribute, with emotions and memories of betrayal, hatred and fondness battling in her mind.

Katniss now possesses a bow and arrows and feels that she is 'no longer merely prey that runs and hides or takes desperate measures' (p.239). Taking a more proactive approach makes her feel as if she's back home, like the natural hunter that she is – though now her prey is fellow human beings.

Even though Rue is not considered a strong player in the game – 'I can almost hear Haymitch groaning as I team up with this wispy child' – Katniss chooses to form an alliance with her because 'she's a survivor' and reminds her of her sister, Prim (p.244). Katniss is more concerned about her principles and doing what she thinks is right than listening to the opinions of others, displaying her strength of character.

Q What are the similarities between Rue and Prim? How do you think Prim would have fared in the arena if Katniss hadn't volunteered in her place?

Chapter 16 (pp.251–67)

Summary: *Katniss and Rue plan to destroy the Careers' supplies at the Cornucopia; they split up, with Katniss going to the Cornucopia itself and Rue luring the Careers away from it; Katniss realises the supplies are surrounded by landmines, and makes them explode through the clever use of her arrows.*

The years in which the Career Tributes have not been able to protect the supplies provided by the Gamemakers are 'usually the years that tributes from other districts have won' – that is because they 'don't know how to be hungry' or how to hunt in the way that tributes like Katniss can (p.252). Thus, targeting their one source of food forms the crux of Katniss' offensive plan.

While survival is understandably the greatest concern and preoccupation in the mind of the tributes, another factor they must contend with is being away from home and their loved ones. Now that Katniss has had breathing space from the onslaught of attacks in the arena, she realises 'for the first time, how very lonely [she's] been in the arena' (p.252). Though she is viewed by some, like Haymitch, as a surly loner, she is shown to be a sociable person who is always around people back in District 12 – at home with her sister, in the woods with Gale and at the Hub with her fellow townspeople.

Q How does taking the offensive give Katniss a greater sense of control? Does she truly have any control in the arena?

Chapter 17 (pp.268–81)

Summary: *Katniss' hearing is damaged in the explosion; the Careers return, and Cato kills the boy from District 3 in anger; Foxface picks over the ruins; Katniss returns to the rendezvous point but can't find Rue, so searches for her; Rue is killed.*

Katniss realises she can't stay where she is, out in the open: 'Not only will I face death, it's sure to be a long and painful one at Cato's hand' (p.270). The rivalry between her and Cato is developing into an important one, helping to build tension towards their inevitable showdown.

Katniss considers having Foxface, a wily tribute, join her alliance, but believes that she would knife her in the back. Katniss is beginning to think in more animalistic, violent ways, noting that 'this might be an excellent time to shoot her' (p.275). This is the type of mentality that is often needed to survive and win the Games.

While looking for Rue, Katniss hears her cry out, which she describes as 'a child's scream' (p.280), and runs to the sound to find Rue trapped in a net. Readers are reminded that the tributes are all children (some, like Rue, younger than others) – a fact that can sometimes be forgotten when violence and death is depicted as a normality in the arena. This is exemplified by the jarring description of Rue being speared, which ends the chapter on a harrowing note.

Q How does Collins keep up an action-packed pace throughout the novel?

Chapter 18 (pp.282–96)

Summary: *Katniss kills Rue's murderer, the boy from District 1, by shooting an arrow into his neck; Katniss comforts Rue in her last moments, then covers her in flowers after her death; Claudius Templesmith announces that there can be two winners of the Games if they are from the same district.*

The chapter begins on a brutal note: 'The boy from District 1 dies before he can pull out the spear' (p.282). Driven by her affection for Rue, and anger at seeing her in danger, Katniss has killed someone with intent for the first time. She later reflects on the moral implications of her actions, but at the time she goes straight to Rue, comforting her in her dying moments. She promises her that she's 'going to win for both of [them] now' (p.283) and sings her a lullaby as she dies. This is one of the saddest, tenderest scenes of the whole book, and highlights the deep-felt human emotions that are at play for these characters.

Katniss 'can't bring [herself] to leave [Rue] like this' (p.285), so first she covers Rue in flowers and then makes the sign with the three middle fingers of her left hand before leaving her. This is a clear act of rebellion against the Capitol and results in her receiving a loaf of bread from District 11, Rue's district: 'this is a first. A district gift to a tribute who's not your own' (p.289). These are early signs of the districts banding together in open rebellion against the Capitol and the Games, an idea that is explored later in the series.

Q What do you think are the psychological consequences for Katniss of having intentionally killed another human for the first time?

Q How important is Rue's death in galvanising Katniss to want to win the Games?

PART III – The Victor

Chapter 19 (pp.299–317)

Summary: *Katniss finds Peeta, who is badly wounded; she tries to help him recover and finds them shelter in a cave.*

Now that she knows both she and Peeta can win the Games, Katniss goes in search of him, as 'it just makes sense to protect each other' (p.299). The only other tributes who could benefit from the rule change announced at the end of the previous chapter are Cato and Clove from District 2, pitting them in direct competition with Katniss and Peeta. However, Katniss surmises that the primary reason for the rule change is that the romance between her and Peeta 'must be so popular with the audience that condemning it would jeopardize the success of the Games' (p.300).

Katniss' strategic mind is on display throughout the course of the novel; in this chapter, she makes a fire to 'confuse [her] enemies' minds' (p.303). Though we haven't seen much of Peeta in the arena up until now, he shows off his own set of skills through his camouflage, so well done that Katniss cannot see him unless he opens his eyes (p.305). Much in the same way that Katniss' skills as a hunter and gatherer back home have helped her to survive, so too have Peeta's skills working at his family bakery.

Q How does this chapter show a different side to Katniss?

Chapter 20 (pp.318–37)

Summary: *Peeta's condition worsens, as Katniss realises he has blood poisoning; she tells him about a happy memory; Claudius announces that there will be a feast, with something that each tribute needs; Katniss gives Peeta sleep syrup and goes to the feast against his wishes.*

While she has only had to worry about herself for much of the Games, Katniss is now tied to a wounded ally, a fact of which she is acutely aware: 'I've made myself far more vulnerable than when I was alone' (p.319). She is unable to do the things that she would want to do to ensure her survival, such as hide out in trees at night or hunt during the day. But she remains loyal and true to her word, sticking by Peeta's side even though it puts her life in greater jeopardy.

Q How does Collins create tension between and intrigue about Katniss' two romantic interests?

Chapter 21 (pp.338–52)

Summary: *Katniss goes to the Cornucopia, where she is attacked by Clove; she is saved by Thresh, who bashes in Clove's skull for killing Rue; Thresh lets Katniss go because she helped Rue; Katniss returns to the cave and gives Peeta the medicine before she passes out.*

The narrative picks up pace considerably in this chapter, as Katniss faces the threat of two fellow tributes. The scene of her almost being killed by Clove is particularly arresting, as it places the protagonist right at the edge of death and a potential end to the story. As is often the case when Katniss is placed under extreme duress, her mind turns to Prim and Rue. While Prim evokes feelings of tender love in Katniss, the thought of Rue and her death provokes anger and vengeance: Clove's 'comment about Rue has filled [her] with fury' (p.347). This gives readers a glimpse into Katniss' sensibilities and motivations.

Katniss' friendship and alliance with Rue again prove to be imperative. Not only does it spur Katniss to action, but it also protects her from the wrath of Thresh, Rue's fellow District 11 tribute, who lets her go 'just this one time' (p.350) because she has shown kindness to one of his own.

Q Katniss comments that 'maybe Foxface is the real opponent here' (p.344). Who do you think Katniss' greatest opponent is?

Chapter 22 (pp.353–68)

Summary: *Peeta looks after Katniss; they discuss their feelings.*

This is a relatively quiet chapter, one that focuses on the emotional depth of Katniss and Peeta's growing relationship. Peeta again displays his soft and caring nature, described by Katniss as being 'all gentleness' (p.354), while Katniss allows her guard to drop and to show a more vulnerable side, telling Peeta 'plaintively, like a small child', 'I want to go home' (p.357).

While Katniss is trying to process her growing feelings for Peeta, she is sure of one thing: she does 'not want to lose the boy with the bread' (p.362). However, she is unable to allow herself to fully embrace the moment because she knows she is on camera. She shares her thought, 'whatever I'm feeling, it's no one's business but mine' (p.362).

The romantic relationship at the heart of the novel blossoms in this chapter, as Katniss begins to reciprocate Peeta's feelings. When they kiss again, she notes, 'this is the first kiss where I actually feel a stirring inside my chest' (p.362). It is not simply kissing that progresses their relationship but the intimacy they are sharing, both physically and emotionally. When Peeta holds Katniss, she remarks, 'since my father died and I stopped trusting my mother, no one else's arms have made me feel this safe' (p.363). Not only is Peeta providing her a sense of security she hasn't felt since she was a young child, but he is also helping her to process and overcome her past trauma.

Q Katniss notes that she's 'not as smooth with words as Peeta' (p.361). How important are words in the Games?

Chapter 23 (pp.369–88)

Summary: *Katniss and Peeta hunt and gather; they find out Thresh is dead; Foxface dies after consuming nightlock berries.*

This chapter provides a brief moment of levity in the story. Katniss and Peeta joke about how their future will look if they win: 'But then, our only neighbour will be Haymitch!' (p.371). This is a reminder of their childlike humour and fun personalities, which have been dampened by the inhumane environment in which they find themselves.

Katniss is consumed by existential questions pertaining to the meaning of life after the Games. She wonders who she will be if she longer needs to hunt and gather food, tasks that took up all her time and attention prior to the Games: 'Take that away and I'm not really sure who I am, what my identity is' (p.378). She considers the example of Haymitch, whose life is ridiculed by citizens of Panem, and declares that she doesn't 'want to end up like that' (p.378).

Key point

The cycle of violence and death does not end in the arena, even if Katniss and Peeta survive this year's Games. If they are victorious, they will be tasked with mentoring the new tributes from District 12 each year, forced to watch them go through the same torment they are experiencing now. Katniss notes that 'it must be hell to mentor two kids and then watch them die' (p.373), as Haymitch has had to do every year since winning. Furthermore, Katniss declares that she does not want to 'risk bringing a child into the world' (p.378) because they may end up being selected to go into the arena.

Q What are your impressions of Haymitch? Does this chapter help to shed perspective on his struggles?

Chapter 24 (pp.389–401)

Summary: *Katniss, Peeta and Cato are driven to the lake for the final battle; muttations are unleashed on the tributes.*

For the first time since entering the arena, Katniss and Peeta have the upper hand: they outnumber the last remaining tribute, Cato. With so few tributes, the Gamemakers drive them together for the climactic final battle, which Katniss considers as having been inevitable right from the start; 'And really, wasn't [Cato] always the one to kill?' (p.397).

Q Consider the following quote: 'It's not much, but out here in the wilderness, it's the closest thing we have to a home' (p.393). What is the significance of home for the characters in the arena?

Chapter 25 (pp.402–19)

Summary: *Katniss, Peeta and Cato seek refuge at the Cornucopia; Katniss and Peeta outmanoeuvre Cato, and he is savaged by the muttations; Katniss kills Cato with an arrow; when it is announced that the rules have changed back, and there can be only one winner, she and Peeta prepare to eat the poisonous berries to defy the Capitol; Claudius suddenly declares them the winners of the Games.*

This is the final scene in the arena, the ultimate confrontation between the remaining tributes. But the Gamemakers want even greater drama, so have unleashed a set of mutated creatures (muttations) created by mixing the DNA of the dead tributes with wolves. Here, the frightening power and capabilities of the Capitol are shown in full, reinforcing its strength in comparison to the districts.

The battle between Katniss and Cato ends in the former's favour, with Katniss shooting Cato's hand as he tries to use Peeta as a shield. However, it is the muttations that end up savaging him, a process that is dragged on by the Gamemakers because 'no viewer could turn away from the show now ... this is the final word in entertainment' (p.412).

The Gamemakers reverse their earlier decision allowing two winners from the same district, showing their two-faced nature – though this comes as no surprise to Katniss, who realises that 'they never intended to let us both live' (p.416). When this announcement is made by Claudius, Katniss instinctively aims an arrow at Peeta just as he throws his knife into the river. This reflex to kill her ally and romantic interest to save herself may be viewed negatively, as shown in her face burning with 'shame' (p.416); however, it reflects the instinct of humans to want to live and shows that Katniss has much to live for.

Q Does the climax reflect the build-up of tension over the course of the novel or does it feel anticlimactic?

Chapter 26 (pp.420–36)

Summary: *Katniss and Peeta are taken back to the Capitol; Peeta is ferried away by doctors; Haymitch warns Katniss that she is still in danger.*

Although she is now free from the threat of the Games, Katniss still has an adversarial mindset; when the doctors take Peeta from her, she sees them 'as just one more threat' (p.421). This is common for survivors of war or conflict, who often struggle to readjust to ordinary life.

When Katniss sees herself in the mirror, she is shocked by what she sees: 'it's my own face reflecting back in the glass. Wild eyes, hollow cheeks, my hair in a tangled mat. Rabid. Feral' (p.422). This vivid picture emblemises the struggle she has had to endure, so intense and horrific that she can barely recognise the girl staring back at her.

While Katniss would have assumed she was safe after winning the Games, Haymitch warns her that she's 'in trouble' for 'showing [the Capitol] up in the arena' (p.433). By performing acts that could be construed as rebellious – covering Rue in flowers, suggesting eating the poisonous berries – Katniss has placed not only herself in harm's way, but also her family and the people of District 12. Here, Collins is setting up the main tension of the subsequent books in the series.

Q This chapter ends with Katniss suggesting that 'the most dangerous part of the Hunger Games is about to begin' (p.436). What does she mean by this?

Chapter 27 (pp.437–54)

Summary: *Katniss and Peeta are interviewed by Caesar; they appear to convince the Capitol that their final act in the arena was not one of rebellion; Peeta discovers that Katniss' feelings towards him were an act.*

Throughout Katniss' interview with Caesar, footage of the Games and the gruesome deaths of the other tributes is shown. This is triggering for Katniss, who does 'not want to watch [her] twenty-two fellow tributes die' (p.439). Mimicking reality television, these highlights have been put together by editors who control the story that is told to the masses: 'Whoever puts together the highlights has to choose what sort of story to tell. This year, for the first time, they tell a love story' (p.440). This reinforces the control exerted by the Capitol on all aspects of the Games.

Thus, the citizens of Panem must play along with the Capitol's narrative in order to ensure their own safety. For Katniss, she is faced with such a moment in the interview, where she must convince everyone that she 'went so crazy at the idea of losing Peeta that [she couldn't] be held responsible for [her] actions' (p.449). Katniss manages to pull off the image of a love-obsessed young girl, enough to keep her out of immediate danger.

Q How has Katniss changed as a character from the start of the novel?

Q How does the ending set up the events of the next book in the series?

CHARACTERS & RELATIONSHIPS

Katniss Everdeen

Key quotes

'Besides, it isn't in my nature to go down without a fight, even when things seem insurmountable.' (p.44)

'No one will forget me. Not my look, not my name. Katniss. The girl who was on fire.' (p.85)

'I begin transforming back into myself. Katniss Everdeen. A girl who lives in the Seam. Hunts in the woods. Trades in the Hob.' (p.450)

Katniss Everdeen is the sixteen-year-old protagonist and narrator of the novel. She is a character with a range of complex emotions, and can be described as brave, headstrong, clever, logical, passionate, empathetic, rebellious and loyal.

Katniss is initially portrayed as tough and even perhaps cruel, as she recollects trying to drown a stray cat her sister brought home years ago. The reason for wanting to do this, however, is pragmatic; as she explains, 'The last thing I needed was another mouth to feed' (p.4). She eventually relents after her sister cries and begs to keep him, foreshadowing Katniss' naturally sensitive and sympathetic tendencies. It is often her interactions with her sister that show her softer side, such as being made to laugh in a way that 'only Prim can draw out of me' (p.18). She is also fiercely protective of Prim, volunteering to take her place in the Hunger Games, thus setting the plot of the novel in motion.

Much of Katniss' stoic sensibilities can be traced back to her traumatic past. Not only does she lose her father at a young age, but 'a mother as well' (p.32), who becomes an invalid following the death of her husband. Katniss 'took over as head of the family' (p.32), forced to take care of her younger sister and provide food for the family by hunting and entering her name additional times in the reaping, to receive tesserae (extra provisions). Not only does this present a psychological burden, but it also results in emotional barriers, as Katniss feels the need to 'put up a wall to protect [herself] from needing her' mother (p.64). Although she has a tense relationship with her mother, Katniss shows that she is a person who is willing to change and grow: 'I'm trying to get past rejecting offers of help from her' (pp.17–18).

The effects of her childhood trauma are far-reaching. She is afraid to open herself up to others and be vulnerable, often turning her 'features into an indifferent mask so that no one could ever read [her] thoughts' (p.7). Perhaps fearful of losing another loved one and getting hurt again, she does not pursue romantic relationships and proclaims that she 'never wants to have kids' (p.11) – also reflecting that she doesn't want to be responsible for bringing children into the world who might suffer a difficult childhood like hers and be chosen to compete in the Games.

Key point

Katniss' primary motivation throughout the novel is her innate desire to survive. Growing up in the impoverished District 12, she learned to be resourceful and skilled in hunting, talents that serve her well in the arena. This survival instinct drives many of her actions throughout the book and is linked to her tenacious and resilient nature, exemplified in her comment that 'pity does not get you aid. Admiration at your refusal to give in does' (p.217).

Throughout the Games, Katniss exhibits resilience, intelligence and compassion. Despite numerous setbacks and injuries in the arena, she continues to look ahead and fight for her survival, never giving up. She is able to keep herself alive and outwit several of her competitors through her quick thinking and logical mindset: 'There is a solution to this, I know there is, if I can only focus hard enough' (p.266). She is able to communicate with Haymitch through her actions in the arena – for example, showing affection to Peeta in return for food – and follows the native wildlife when the fire breaks out in the woods: 'I trust their sense of direction because their instincts are sharper than mine' (p.208). Despite possessing the mindset of a hunter and killing several other tributes, Katniss does not allow the Games to turn her into a callous murderer. She maintains her morals and sense of compassion throughout, shown in the way she interacts with and cares for Rue, nurses Peeta back to health and puts Cato out of his misery (p.414).

Another important aspect of Katniss' character is her rebellious nature, both in terms of her actions and what she comes to represent for the people of Panem. At home, she hunts in the forest outside of District 12 even though it is illegal and sells her wares in the district's black market. These are relatively minor indiscretions compared to her actions in the arena. By covering Rue's dead body in flowers, Katniss displays a solidarity between the districts that the Capitol is adamant about stamping out. Also, with her plan that she and Peeta would eat the poisonous nightlock berries, ensuring that there would be no victor, Katniss shows the Gamemakers to be fools, which sets in motion a battle for control of the nation that is explored in the subsequent books in the series.

Peeta Mellark

Key quotes

'I don't want them to change me in there. Turn me into some kind of monster that I'm not.' (p.171)

'Only I keep wishing I could think of a way to ... to show the Capitol they don't own me. That I'm more than just a piece in their Games.' (p.172)

'It's not that Peeta's soft exactly, and he's proved he's not a coward. But there are things you don't question too much ... when your home always smells like baking bread.' (p.360)

Described as being of 'medium height', 'stocky build', with 'ashy blond hair' (p.31), Peeta is the male tribute from District 12 and Katniss' primary love interest throughout the novel. He is the baker's son, a role that has built him into a sturdy young man: 'All those years of having enough to eat and hauling bread trays around have made him broad-shouldered and strong' (p.49).

Peeta is known for his kindness, compassion and selflessness. He has a gentle and caring nature, which makes him well-liked by those around him; for example, he selflessly cares for Haymitch when he falls in his own vomit. Not only is he friendly and easygoing, but he is also well-spoken, allowing him to charm the Capitol crowd during his interviews.

Despite the harsh and brutal world of the Hunger Games, Peeta maintains his moral compass and refuses to let the brutality of the Games change who he is at his core. While Katniss has 'been ruminating on the availability of trees' prior to the start of the Games, Peeta 'has been struggling with how to maintain his identity', 'his purity of self' (p.171). He is more concerned about not turning into a 'monster' (p.171) than about winning the Games, and his moral character never appears to waver throughout the novel.

Peeta and Katniss

One of the key relationships at the heart of the book is between Peeta and Katniss. Peeta's characterisation is a direct result of Katniss' narration, so the reader learns about him primarily through their burgeoning romance. Katniss recounts her first meeting with him, when he risked a beating to give her deliberately burned bread, saying, 'It's weird, how much he's noticed me ... And apparently, I have not been as oblivious to him as I imagined, either ... I have kept track of the boy with the bread' (p.113).

Peeta has secretly harboured a flame for Katniss since their first meeting, and she has seemed oblivious to his feelings, showing little interest in romantic relationships in general. It is only once they begin spending time together after having been selected as tributes that Katniss considers Peeta in a different light: 'he gives me a smile that seems so genuinely sweet with just the right touch of shyness that unexpected warmth rushes through me' (p.88). However, her feelings are tempered by the knowledge that they cannot both survive the

Games: 'at some point, we're going to have to knock it off and accept we're bitter adversaries' (p.113).

In the arena, Katniss initially feels betrayed when it looks as though Peeta has joined with the Career Tributes; however, she soon learns this is all a ploy and that he is looking out for her. As the Games progress, Katniss and Peeta's bond deepens. They share intimate moments, nursing each other back to health, and present themselves as star-crossed lovers to the Capitol audience, which helps them gain sponsors and support. Katniss begins to realise her feelings for Peeta but remains conflicted, partly because of her unnamed relationship with Gale back home, which elicits jealousy from Peeta: 'She's just worried about her boyfriend' (p.165).

Gale Hawthorn

Key quotes

'He's good-looking, he's strong enough to handle the work in the mines, and he can hunt.' (p.12)

'That was the first time I ever saw him smile. It transformed him from someone menacing to someone you wished you knew.' (p.135)

'I can't help comparing what I have with Gale to what I'm pretending to have with Peeta.' (p.136)

'But he turned into so much more than a hunting partner. He became my confidant, someone with whom I could share thoughts I could never voice inside the fence. In exchange, he trusted me with his.' (p.136)

Gale is a character who appears only briefly in the action of the novel, but whose presence contributes to the narrative nonetheless, through the lens of the protagonist. Though he is described as looking like Katniss' 'brother' (p.9), he is presented as Katniss' other love interest in the book.

While Katniss notes that 'there's never been anything romantic between Gale and [her]' (p.11) at the start of the novel, she also recognises that calling him a friend is 'too casual a word for what Gale is to [her]' (p.136). In the Capitol she muses, 'I wonder if Gale is in the woods yet' (p.132) and, once in the arena, she continues to reflect on the nature of their relationship, particularly in the context of her 'romance' with Peeta. When Katniss expresses affection to Peeta in the arena, in order to gain food and medicine from Haymitch and the sponsors watching, she instantly thinks of how this will be perceived by Gale.

Unlike Peeta, Gale shares many interests and similarities with Katniss. They hunt together in the woods, they must support their families as the eldest siblings and they harbour rebellious thoughts about the Capitol. They share a special connection, with Katniss describing him as 'the only person with whom I can be myself' (p.7) and as providing 'a sense of security I'd lacked since my father's death' (p.135).

Although he is a pragmatist, working hard within the system – and sometimes outside of it – he is also a dreamer. He asks Katniss to run away with him at the start of the novel (p.10), which Katniss references towards the end of the novel: 'Gale's not my boyfriend, but would he be, if I opened that door? He talked about us running away together' (p.341).

The Career Tributes

Key quotes

'I look around at the Career Tributes, who are showing off, clearly trying to intimidate the field.' (p.116)

'Career Tributes are overly vicious, arrogant, better fed, but only because they're the Capitol's lapdogs. Universally, solidly hated by all but those from their own districts.' (p.196)

'I wonder now if Cato might not be entirely sane.' (p.394)

Tributes from the districts closest to the Capitol are called Career Tributes, or Careers. Though there are several members of the group, the ones who are most fleshed out as characters in their own right are Cato and Clove from District 2; they pose the greatest danger to Katniss in the arena.

Career Tributes are chosen at a young age and are put through rigorous training in combat, survival skills and strategy. They are often mentored by previous victors from their districts, a benefit that poorer districts with fewer winners do not have: 'It's technically against the rules to train tributes before they reach the Capitol, but it happens every year' (p.115).

In the novel, these tributes are shown to lack compassion and empathy, characterised instead as killing machines who 'project arrogance and brutality' (p.116). They are known for their aggressive and ruthless tactics in the arena; they are often the first to engage in combat and are skilled in using weapons and traps.

Due to her strong showing prior to the start of the Games, Katniss is placed in direct competition with the Career Tributes, and Cato in particular. This is only exacerbated when she drops a tracker-jacker nest on them while they sleep, killing two and injuring the others in the process. Cato, who is clearly vindictive and vengeful, takes personal offence at this and seeks retribution, telling the others, 'When we find her, I kill her in my own way, and no one interferes' (p.262). Ultimately, Katniss and Peeta emerge victorious in the battle with the Career Tributes, showing how logic and thinking can prevail over brawn.

Primrose 'Prim' Everdeen

Key quotes

'How could I leave Prim, who is the only person in the world I'm certain I love?' (p.11)

'People deal with me, but they are genuinely fond of Prim.' (p.46)

'As usual, it's the thought of Prim's anxious face as she watches me on the screens back home that breaks me from my lethargy.' (p.290)

Though she only appears in the first two chapters, twelve-year-old Prim plays a significant role in the plot of the book. When her name is selected at the reaping, her older sister Katniss immediately volunteers to take her place, thus setting the events of the novel in motion.

Prim is portrayed as a kind-hearted, gentle and nurturing young girl. She is compassionate and cares deeply for both people and animals, and her tender nature is one of the reasons she is drawn to healing and medicine. Katniss notes while nursing Peeta's injuries in the arena, 'ironically, at this point in the Games, my little sister would be of far more use to Peeta than I am' (p.311).

She is depicted as the antithesis to Katniss: whereas Katniss is pragmatic and detached, Prim is emotional and soft. Katniss is a hunter, Prim a healer. When Katniss tries to teach her how to hunt, Prim cries after her sister shoots an animal, and talks about 'how we might be able to heal it if we got it home soon enough' (p.42). Despite their binary character traits, the sisters love each other deeply, and Katniss leaving to fight in the Games is profoundly felt.

Key point

The character of Prim is mirrored in the girl tribute from District 11, Rue, with whom Katniss develops a similar sisterly bond. When she first notices Rue in the training centre, Katniss notes she 'reminded [her] so of Prim' (p.120); the two eventually develop an alliance in the arena, as Rue becomes Katniss' stand-in sister. In Rue's final moments, she asks Katniss to sing to her, and Katniss conflates her with Prim, who is the only person she would sing for, saying, 'But if this is Prim's, I mean, Rue's last request, I have to at least try' (p.283).

Haymitch Abernathy

Key quotes

'Well, what's this ... Did I actually get a pair of fighters this year?' (p.69)

'I think of Haymitch, with all his money. What did his life become? He lives alone, no wife or children, most of his waking hours drunk. I don't want to end up like that.' (p.378)

'I run for them and surprise even myself when I launch into Haymitch's arms first. When he whispers in my ear, "Nice job, sweetheart," it doesn't sound sarcastic.' (p.427)

Haymitch is introduced as the only living victor from District 12, having won the 50th Hunger Games. His character is initially depicted as 'the laughing stock of Panem' (p.23) because of his constant drunken antics since winning the Games. His fiery, stubborn disposition is similar to Katniss – Peeta notes that they're 'just alike' (p.313) – and the two develop a love-hate father-daughter relationship throughout the course of the novel.

The importance of Haymitch's character, along with mentors more broadly, is alluded to at the start of the novel. As Effie notes, 'your mentor is your lifeline to the world in these Games. The one who advises you, lines up your sponsors, and dictates the presentation of any gifts. Haymitch can well be the difference between your life and your death!' (p.56). Initially, this is set up to be a potential obstacle for Katniss and Peeta, as Haymitch has a reputation for being a drunkard – though, as the novel progresses, we learn that first impressions are not always what they seem.

As Katniss begins to reflect on life after the Games, she realises she will have to mentor the tributes from her district, saying, 'It must be hell to mentor two kids and then watch them die' (p.373). This gives her a newfound perspective on Haymitch, who likely turned to drinking because 'it got unbearable' (p.373). His alcoholism is both a character flaw and a symbol of the toll that the Hunger Games takes on its victors, highlighting the prolonged effect of trauma on mental wellbeing. His cynical and sarcastic attitude serves as a further defence mechanism, shielding him from the pain and harsh realities of the Capitol's oppression.

Haymitch agrees to assist Katniss and Peeta after seeing their fiery temperaments. He uses his knowledge of the Games to guide them through the interview and training processes, helping them to make a significant impact on viewers by casting them as star-crossed lovers. This eventually paves the way for a rule change that allows both of them to win the Games. Though he was initially indifferent to Katniss and Peeta, he eventually grows to care for them and is 'actually bent on keeping [them] alive' (p.445), even after the Games have finished and his official duties as mentor have ended.

THEMES, IDEAS & VALUES

Oppression and rebellion

Key quotes

'Look how we take your children and sacrifice them and there's nothing you can do. If you lift a finger, we will destroy every last one of you. Just as we did in District Thirteen.' (p.22)

'I want to do something, right here, right now, to shame them, to make them accountable, to show the Capitol that whatever they do or force us to do there is a part of every tribute they can't own. That Rue was more than a piece in their Games. And so am I.' (p.286)

'But the Hunger Games are their weapon and you are not supposed to be able to defeat it.' (p.435)

Set in a dystopian world in which a brutalist regime reigns over its citizens, the novel is undeniably focused on the themes of oppression and rebellion. Mirroring the real-world fascist regimes of Hitler's Germany, Stalin's Russia, Mao Zedong's China and Jong-un's North Korea, the Capitol enforces its rule over the nation of Panem through surveillance, manipulation, violence, propaganda and – its ultimate weapon – the annual Hunger Games.

Oppression

Following 'droughts', 'storms', 'fires', 'encroaching seas' and a 'brutal war', the Capitol was established, ringed by thirteen districts; however, a failed uprising against the Capitol by the districts (a time known as 'the Dark Days') led to the obliteration of the thirteenth district and the establishment of 'the Hunger Games' (p.21). While the Hunger Games is the most prominent means of oppression, it is merely one tool used by a totalitarian regime to subjugate its citizens and quell any form of further rebellion.

One of these tools is constant surveillance. Not only does this allow the Capitol to catch, prosecute and punish wrongdoers, but it also instils fear and obedience in citizens, who are wary of acting outside of the law. The Capitol deploys hovercrafts and cameras equipped with advanced technology to monitor the activities of the residents in the districts. These surveillance tools are used to keep an eye on people's movements, actions and conversations, ensuring that not even a bad word can be said about those in power; Gale and Katniss only feel comfortable criticising the Capitol when they are alone in the woods, outside the boundaries of the districts, where no one can reasonably hear them. The Peacekeepers, essentially the Capitol's enforcers, also patrol the districts and ensure that the residents comply with Capitol rules, reporting any suspicious or rebellious behaviour back to the Capitol. At events such as the reaping, in which attendance is mandatory for everyone, the Capitol can 'keep tabs on the [whole] population' (p.19).

Key point

No form of oppression is absolute – it is dependent on the loyalty of its enforcers. Many citizens in the districts flout the rules, primarily through hunting and trading at the Hob, and most of the Peacekeepers 'turn a blind eye to the few of [those] who hunt because they're as hungry for fresh meat as anybody is' (p.6), highlighting that individual desires and needs trump allegiance to a faraway government.

Another tool of oppression used by the Capitol is violence, and this is apparent in the day-to-day life of those in the districts. The Capitol's Peacekeepers, armed enforcers stationed in each district, maintain a climate of constant fear through both the threat and the display of violence. As Rue explains to Katniss in the arena, if you eat the crops you grow in District 11, 'they whip you and make everyone else watch' (p.245). Katniss herself reveals the potential ramifications for breaking the law, saying, 'I could be shot on a daily basis for hunting, but the appetites of those in charge protect me. Not everyone can claim the same' (p.20).

The greatest display of violence and psychological warfare is, of course, the Hunger Games: they take 'the kids from our districts, forcing them to kill one another while we watch – this is the Capitol's way of reminding us how totally we are at their mercy' (p.22). Each year, the citizens must watch as children from their districts are brutally murdered on their screens, starve to death, or suffer a host of other gruesome deaths in the arena. The Games are inhumane and grisly, described as a 'sport' (p.214) that those in the Capitol enjoy as a form of entertainment.

The Games and the events surrounding them are also used as a form of propaganda, to help portray the Capitol as a utopian society, rich in luxury, fashion, food and entertainment, to which the districts can aspire. The Games are a televised spectacle, with every aspect of the event carefully curated for maximum entertainment value. The tributes' backstories, interviews and public appearances are all manipulated by the Capitol to create certain narratives and evoke specific emotions from the audience. As Katniss notes, 'Whoever puts together the highlights has to choose what sort of story to tell' (p.440). The Capitol also forces the winners of the Games to help further its propaganda machine. After winning the Games, Katniss and Peeta must follow the tradition of the victors being paraded around the districts. 'It's the Capitol's way of reminding people that the Hunger Games never really go away' (p.449), as well as reminding the winners that they have no more power than they did before they participated in the Games.

Rebellion

On the surface, it seems that the Capitol's control over the districts is absolute, with no avenue for rebellion; however, Katniss' actions in the arena show that there are small but powerful ways to galvanise the people and let them know that they will not remain a subjugated class forever.

The first sign of rebellion occurs early in the novel, when Katniss becomes the tribute for District 12 after volunteering to save her sister. Instead of applauding as they normally would do, the onlookers 'take part in the boldest form of dissent they can manage. Silence. Which says we do not agree. We do not condone. All of this is wrong' (pp.28–9). They then touch the middle three fingers of their left hand to their lips and hold it out to Katniss, a symbol that represents rebellion throughout the series. Though they cannot change the outcome of the reaping, the people of District 12 are letting the Capitol know what they think about their inhumane and totalitarian regime, a powerful gesture when the threat of violence always lingers.

Katniss displays a defiant lack of care about the Gamemakers and what they represent when she shoots an arrow in their direction during the training sessions. They pass this off as a sign of a fiery tribute who will put on a good show in the arena and so give her a high score, but this act alludes to the willingness of Katniss to challenge the status quo.

In the arena, this defiant streak continues through Katniss' friendship with Rue. Tributes from competing districts rarely befriend each other in the arena, other than to form superficial alliances that will eventually need to end because there is generally only one winner. However, Katniss and Rue develop a real bond and share with each other stories of their lives in their respective districts. Even something as seemingly innocuous as this can be rebellious. Katniss realises this, noting that 'they don't want people in different districts to know about one another' (p.246) because this can sow the seeds of rebellion, as seen in the example of District 13.

Katniss is urged to express her defiance following Rue's death, as she is forced 'to confront [her] own fury against the cruelty, the injustice they inflict upon us' and it leads her to wonder whether there is any way 'to take revenge on the Capitol' (p.286). Katniss decides to cover Rue's body in flowers, as a show of respect, an act that is omitted during the final interview 'because even that smacks of rebellion' (p.441).

The ultimate act of rebellion occurs towards the end of the book, when Katniss and Peeta prepare to eat poisonous berries and deprive the Gamemakers of a victor. As Haymitch notes, 'the Hunger Games are their weapon and you are not supposed to be able to defeat it' (p.435). Katniss' logic and daring are in direct defiance of the Capitol and, while it places her in danger following the Games, she has shown her fellow citizens that there are ways to rebel against and challenge the oppressive rule of the Capitol government.

Social inequality

Key quotes

'The reaping system is unfair, with the poor getting the worst of it.' (p.15)

'A way to plant hatred between the starving workers of the Seam and those who can generally count on supper; and thereby ensure we will never trust one another.' (p.16)

'It's to the Capitol's advantage to have us divided among ourselves ...' (p.16)

'Electricity in District 12 comes and goes; usually we only have it a few hours a day. Often the evenings are spent in candlelight ... But here there would be no shortage. Ever.' (p.98)

Collins replicates the vastly expanding rich–poor divide in the US through the juxtaposition of the obscenely wealthy Capitol and the impoverished districts. This stark division highlights the inequality that can arise in a capitalist system, where a small elite class benefits at the expense of the working class, a concept that Collins seems to be critiquing.

The Capitol is the seat of power and luxury, known for its high living standards, opulent architecture, lavish food and eccentric fashion; in contrast, the districts are impoverished and oppressed, with a lack of adequate food and harsh working conditions. As Katniss notes, 'They do surgery in the Capitol, to make people appear younger and thinner. In District 12, looking old is something of an achievement since so many people die early' (p.150). Those in the Capitol have the luxury of time and money to worry about their appearance, whereas those in the districts are concerned only with surviving each day.

While the districts are responsible for producing goods and resources for the Capitol, they receive very little of this in return. The Capitol exploits the labour and resources of the districts for its own benefit, leaving the people of the districts struggling to meet their basic needs. When Katniss goes to the Capitol for the first time, she instantly notices the abundance and accessibility of food: 'What must it be like, I wonder, to live in a world where food appears at the press of a button' (p.79). This economic inequality is a driving force behind the resentment felt by the districts.

In order for those in the districts to be able to sustain their families, many of the poorer children opt to submit their names more times for the reaping in exchange for tesserae, which 'is worth a meagre year's supply of grain and oil for one person' (p.15) – for example, Gale has his name entered forty-two times (p.24). They do so even though it increases the chances of being selected to take part in the Games – a very likely death sentence, especially when you are from one of the outer districts and not trained for combat, like the Career Tributes.

Key point

The Capitol uses starvation tactics to further control and divide the populous. When Katniss thinks about questioning what she is taught in school about the history of Panem and the rebellion, she remarks, 'But I don't spend much time thinking about it. Whatever the truth is, I don't see how it will help me get food on the table' (p.51). Citizens are too concerned with securing basic needs such as food to concern themselves with political issues or rebellion.

While those in the districts think primarily about food and survival, those who live in the Capitol think primarily about social standing. At the beginning of the novel, Effie shows no sympathy or care for the tributes of her assigned district; 'everyone knows she's just aching to get bumped up to a better district where they have proper victors, not drunks who molest you in front of the entire nation' (p.23). Though she eventually comes to show some form of compassion towards Katniss and Peeta, one wonders whether this is only because they have performed above expectations for District 12 tributes in the Games.

There is not only social inequality between the Capitol and the districts, but also in the districts themselves. For example, the class division in District 12 is exemplified in the character of Madge, the daughter of the mayor. While she believes it's possible for her name to be chosen in the reaping, Gale coolly tells her, 'You won't be going to the Capitol' (p.14), referring to the fact that she has, at most, five entries compared to his forty-two. Katniss notes how 'it's hard not to resent those who don't have to sign up for tesserae' (p.16), thus exacerbating class divides and leading citizens of the districts to direct their anger towards each other rather than towards the Capitol.

The idea of class divides is also explored in the context of Katniss and Peeta's burgeoning romantic relationship. Discussing how their relationship would be perceived back home, Katniss tells Peeta, 'I'm sure that would thrill your parents, you liking a girl from the Seam' (p.370). Though they are both from the same district, Peeta's family owns a business (a bakery) and would likely identify as middle class, whereas Katniss' family lives in the poor area of town, the Seam, and would likely identify as working class, with her father having been a coalminer. Thus, Panem society places the same importance on social class as our contemporary society does. There are always exceptions to this kind of thinking, however, as shown in Peeta's love for Katniss despite her class, and in Katniss' mother, who 'must have really loved [Katniss' father] to leave her home for the Seam' (p.10).

Survival

Key quotes

'Starvation's not an uncommon fate in District 12.' (p.33)

'But you have to take care, too. You're so fast and brave. Maybe you can win.' (Prim, p.44)

'If there's one rabbit, there could be hundreds just waiting to be snared.' (p.184)

'Despite the risk I took in getting the backpack, I know now it was the right choice. This sleeping bag ... will be invaluable.' (p.189)

The physical aspect of survival is the most immediate concern for the characters in *The Hunger Games*, both inside and outside the arena.

Most of the main characters in the book are from District 12, one of the poorer districts in Panem. They are faced with poor wages, harsh working conditions, poverty and starvation. Furthermore, lack of economic opportunities and resources makes it difficult for residents to improve their standard of living, access education or obtain proper healthcare. The majority of the population works in dangerous and physically demanding conditions, which increases the risk of accidents and health issues; however, 'since almost no one can afford doctors, apothecaries are our healers' (p.9).

Katniss and Gale exemplify the struggles of the children of the poor districts: they illegally hunt beyond the boundaries of the Seam to have enough food to feed their families; they trade at the black market, the Hob; and they put their names multiple times in the reaping to get more tesserae. While they are brave and skilled enough to do these things, they are outliers; most children in District 12, and particularly the Seam, get by on little food and are severely malnourished. Comparing herself to the tributes from the other poor districts during one of their training sessions, Katniss notes that 'the meat and plants from the woods combined with the exertion it took to get them have given [her] a healthier body than most' (p.115).

The extensive knowledge of the wilderness that Katniss develops during these times of hardship also helps to prepare for the hostile environment of the Games. She and the other tributes are placed in an arena filled with deadly traps, extreme temperatures and no easy access to food or water. Katniss must rely on her survival skills, honed through years of hunting in the District 12 woods, to secure food, water and shelter. Her ability to climb trees, run and navigate treacherous terrain gives her an edge over many of the other tributes, and she is also able to hunt animals such as rabbits, using a snare or bow and arrow. Katniss' physical strength and endurance are also central to her survival. She knows when to push herself to the limit and when to conserve energy; though, of course, the demands of the Games are much more excessive than what she is used to back home. When she struggles to find a source of water at the start of the Games, she is left feeling extremely weak, so much so, she says, 'any tribute, even tiny Rue, could take me right now' (p.205). She uses her logic and critical thinking skills to overcome this obstacle, realising that Haymitch is trying to tell her that she is close to a source of water because 'there's only one good reason Haymitch could be withholding water from me' (p.204).

War and morality

Key quotes

'The awful thing is that if I can forget they're people, [killing them] will be no different at all.' (p.48)

'I want to die as myself … I don't want them to change me in there. Turn me into some kind of monster that I'm not.' (Peeta, p.171)

'Because if he dies, I'll never go home, not really. I'll spend the rest of my life in this arena, trying to think my way out.' (p.417)

War and conflict are at the centre of *The Hunger Games*, with much of the action taking place in an arena where the tributes must fight and kill each other in order to survive. A question that often arises in situations such as these is whether it is morally acceptable to kill in order to survive. However, regardless of whether it is deemed acceptable, there are moral and ethical questions that individuals must address for themselves when faced with killing other human beings.

Peeta wrestles with these very questions in the days leading up to the Games. Talking to Katniss, he says, 'I want to die as myself … I don't want them to change me in there. Turn me into some kind of monster that I'm not' (p.171). He is alluding to the idea that people can lose their sense of humanity when they take the life of another human being, regardless of whether it is necessary to stay alive.

Key point

The tributes are no longer described as children but as 'predator[s]' (p.182) who are 'hacking away at one another' (p.183). This visceral image encapsulates how easy it is for humans to turn to violence when their lives are at stake. It also depicts the 'fight' response, an automatic physiological response to danger or threats; the other natural response, 'flight', is shown in Katniss and others fleeing the scene at the start of the Games and heading to the perceived safety of the woods.

Because the story is told through Katniss as protagonist, readers are not made privy to the depth of Peeta's feelings on this issue. When he indirectly kills Foxface when she eats the poisonous nightlock berries he had foraged, we do not get to see how it affects him on an emotional or psychological level. The only information we get is from Katniss, who shares that she doesn't think 'Peeta felt good about killing her, even if it was essential' (p.394).

Katniss is less preoccupied with such questions, though she feels 'inferior' for worrying about the 'availability of trees' while Peeta has been kept awake at night by deep philosophical questions about his identity and moral character (p.171). While she is initially hesitant to take a life, the brutal reality of the Games forces her to confront the moral ambiguity of her actions. Like Peeta, her first kills in the arena are indirect: when she drops the tracker-jacker nest on the Career Tributes, the wasps sting and kill two of the tributes. This act does not impede Katniss' journey through the arena, as she is still consumed with thoughts of her own survival. The hostile environment in which she finds herself even leads her to actively seek to slay her competitors: 'If Cato broke through the trees right now, I wouldn't flee, I'd shoot. I find I'm actually anticipating the moment with pleasure' (p.239).

Moral questions about killing others finally hit home for Katniss when she murders the boy from District 1, moments after he has fatally wounded her friend and ally Rue. Though she is consumed with feelings of sadness and anger over the loss of Rue in the immediate aftermath of this kill, her act of violence eventually comes back to haunt her psyche: 'Then I realize ... he was my first kill ... the boy from District 1 was the first person I knew would die because of my actions' (p.294). She begins questioning the effects of her actions, considering the hurt and pain that must be felt by his family, friends and perhaps 'a girlfriend who really believed he would come back' (p.294). Though she recognises it was a necessary kill, she still expresses regret and sorrow for her part in causing pain to others, indicating that she has not lost her humanity through killing another human being.

Even more complex moral questions arise at the end of the novel, when Katniss and Peeta learn that they cannot both win the Games, as previously indicated by the Gamemakers, and must decide who will survive and who will perish. They each want the other to win, knowing that guilt would overcome them if they were the one to walk out of the arena as the winner: 'I know death right here, right now would be the easier of the two' (p.417).

Ultimately, Katniss concocts a daring plan in which they threaten to eat poisonous berries as a last resort to defy the Capitol's rule that only one tribute can win. This act of defiance is a powerful statement against the Capitol's brutality, but it also raises questions about the morality of suicide as a form of resistance. Ultimately, the Capitol relents and allows both Katniss and Peeta to be declared winners, but the moral ambiguity of their actions lingers.

Suffering as entertainment

Key quotes

'All I can think is how unjust the whole thing is, the Hunger Games. Why am I hopping around like some trained dog trying to please people I hate?' (p.142)

'The audience in the Capitol will be getting bored, claiming that these Games are verging on dullness. This is the one thing the Games must not do.' (p.209)

'No viewer could turn away from the show now. From the Gamemakers' point of view, this is the final word in entertainment.' (p.412)

Another prominent theme in the novel is the idea of suffering as entertainment. While the Hunger Games are primarily a tool used by the Capitol to exert control and oppress its citizens in the districts, they have also become an event that those in the Capitol enjoy as a form of entertainment and sport. They attend pre-Games events such as the interviews with Caesar, bet on who they think will win and sponsor their favourite tributes with items such as food and medicine.

The Capitol glamorises this violence, turning it into a bloodthirsty reality show with sponsors, interviews and fan followings. This glorification of violence desensitises both the Capitol citizens and the readers to the suffering of the tributes, who are mere pawns for entertainment. They are selected through a lottery-like system that emphasises the arbitrary nature of their participation. Once chosen, they undergo a process of transformation, as they are prepped and styled to be visually appealing for the audience, as 'the best-looking tributes always seem to pull more sponsors' (p.70).

Viewers of the Hunger Games find joy in watching the tributes suffer physically, emotionally and psychologically, as they themselves luxuriate in the comfort of their homes. Bloodshed and gore do not disgust them; in fact, the only atrocity that is cautioned against is 'cannibalism', because it 'doesn't play well with the Capitol audience' (p.173).

DIFFERENT INTERPRETATIONS

Different interpretations arise from different responses to a text. Over time, a text will evoke a wide range of responses from its readers, who may come from various social or cultural groups and live in very different places and historical periods. Responses by critics and reviewers can be published in newspapers, journals and books, both online and in print. They can also be expressed in discussions among readers in the media, classrooms, book groups and so on.

While there is no single correct reading or interpretation of a text, it is important to understand that an interpretation is more than a personal opinion – it is the justification of a point of view on the text. To present an interpretation of a text based on your point of view, you must use a logical argument and support it with relevant evidence from the text.

Critical viewpoints

Reviews of *The Hunger Games* have been overwhelmingly positive, though some have noted similarities with other works. It was praised primarily for its plot and character development, as well as its themes.

Stephen King, writing for *Entertainment Weekly*, called it 'a violent, jarring speed-rap of a novel that generates nearly constant suspense' and praised the author as 'an efficient no-nonsense prose stylist with a pleasantly dry sense of humor' (King 2008). In a review for *The New York Times*, John Green wrote that the novel was 'brilliantly plotted and perfectly paced', and that 'the considerable strength of the novel comes in Collins's convincingly detailed world-building and her memorably complex and fascinating heroine'. Though he did also mention that, for the most part, the writing 'described the action and little else' (Green 2008).

Several critics have noted similarities between *The Hunger Games* and Koushun Takami's 1999 novel *Battle Royale*. Susan Dominus of *The New York Times* reports that 'the parallels are striking enough that Collins's work has been savaged on the blogosphere as a baldfaced ripoff' but argued that 'there are enough possible sources for the plot line that the two authors might well have hit on the same basic setup independently' (Dominus 2011).

Two possible interpretations

The following interpretations demonstrate how even directly contrasting viewpoints about a text can be valid, as long as they are supported with evidence from that text.

Interpretation 1: *The Hunger Games* shows that there is only suffering in dystopian societies.

Through her narration, Katniss shows readers what life in Panem is like for those in the districts. And it is a cruel, unforgiving picture.

Those in District 12 suffer starvation, poverty, lack of proper healthcare and harsh working conditions. Most of the citizens of this district are forced to work in the coal mines, and this unsafe working environment often leads to casualties, such as the death of Katniss' father. The run-on effect of losing her father is significant: Katniss' mother is so consumed with grief that she can no longer function as a caring parent to her two children; Katniss must provide for her mother and younger sister, Prim, by illegally hunting in the woods and trading at the black market; Katniss is traumatised by the loss of her father and struggles to show vulnerability to others, for fear of letting them in and then losing them, like she did with her father. Even those who appear to be better off still struggle – for example, despite owning the bakery, Peeta and his family eat only the stale bread that is left over at the end of the day, 'the hard dry loaves that no one else wanted' (p.377).

To make matters worse, there is a staggering level of social inequality in the nation of Panem. The stark contrast between the opulence of the Capitol and the poverty of the districts is a source of suffering for those like Katniss and Gale – 'it's hard not to resent those who don't have to sign up for tesserae' (p.16). The Capitol's extravagant lifestyle is built on the suffering of the districts, which creates a sense of injustice and resentment. They are forced to mine natural resources such as coal and minerals, and grow crops such as wheat, to be used at the Capitol's discretion; as Rue from District 11 points out, if you try to eat the crops you grow 'they whip you and make everyone else watch' (p.245). This is life under an oppressive totalitarian regime.

The most immediate and obvious form of suffering is the physical pain and danger endured by the teenagers selected as tributes for the annual Hunger Games. This event is an atrocious and gruesome display of the Capitol's power over its citizens – 'the Capitol's way of reminding us how totally we are at their mercy' (p.22). The tributes face hunger, dehydration and exposure to extreme weather, and are forced to engage in deadly combat with one another. We watch as Katniss nearly dies of thirst, as Peeta suffers from extreme 'blood poisoning' (p.322) that can only be healed with proper medicine from the Capitol, and, perhaps most gruesomely of all, as Rue is fatally wounded by another tribute and passes away as her friend Katniss sings to her.

It is not only the tributes themselves who suffer, but also their friends and family back home, who are forced to watch every moment telecast on their screens. In contrast, the citizens in the Capitol view the Games as a form of entertainment, which reflects a disturbing desensitisation to the suffering of others. The fact that the suffering and deaths of the tributes are televised for entertainment highlights the society's moral degradation.

Interpretation 2: *The Hunger Games* shows that even in the darkest of circumstances, there is light.

Despite the obvious horrors of the Hunger Games, there are positive aspects that shine through the darkness – namely: resilience, relationships and rebellion.

Katniss' ability to overcome a difficult upbringing, the loss of a parent, poverty and becoming a tribute in the Games shows the importance of a resilient mindset and the power of the human spirit. Her struggles only make her a stronger person. Where her mother crumbles following the death of her husband, Katniss rises to the occasion, providing for both her mother and her younger sister, Prim, by hunting in the woods and trading at the black market. Similarly, in the arena, she adapts to the brutal environment in which she finds herself, strategising to stay alive and facing adversity head-on. Each time she is pushed down – unable to find a source of water, attacked by fireballs, trapped in a tree by the Career Tributes, losing her ally Rue, having to travel with a severely wounded Peeta – she finds a way to overcome the obstacle and push through any discomfort. Her show of resilience is an inspiration to her sister and other young girls in the districts.

Connections formed between the tributes also show that there is good in the world. Though the immediate reaction to the other tributes is adversarial, Katniss' relationship with Rue underscores the importance of human connection in times of hardship. The two tributes form a deep bond and share with one another stories about their respective districts, despite the Capitol not wanting 'people in different districts to know about one another' (p.246). In Rue, Katniss sees her younger sister, Prim, and is thus reminded of the innocence in the world. When Rue is killed, Katniss honours her memory by covering her body with flowers. This act of compassion highlights Katniss' moral strength in a world that encourages cruelty and indifference. It serves as a reminder that, even in the darkest of circumstances, individuals can choose to uphold their moral principles.

Finally, although the people of Panem find themselves living under a despotic government that suppresses its citizens through surveillance, propaganda and violence, there is a growing air of rebellion sparked by Katniss' actions in the arena. In addition to talking about different districts with another tribute and covering Rue's body in flowers before making the gesture of rebellion with her left hand, Katniss also displays her defiant spirit by suggesting to Peeta that they eat the poisonous nightlock berries together and deprive the Gamemakers of a victor. These actions show that totalitarian rule is not absolute and that the power ultimately rests with the people. They are signs of hope for a better future, showing the people of Panem that they will not live in darkness forever.

QUESTIONS & ANSWERS

This section focuses on your own analytical writing on the text, and gives you strategies for producing high-quality responses in your coursework and exam essays.

Essay writing – an overview

An essay on a literary work is a formal and serious piece of writing that presents your point of view on the text, usually in response to a given topic. Your 'point of view' in an essay is your interpretation of the meaning of the text's language, structure, characters, situations and events, supported by detailed analysis of textual evidence.

Analyse – don't summarise

In your essays it is important to avoid simply summarising what happens in a text.

- A **summary** is a description or paraphrase (retelling in different words) of the characters and events. For example: 'Macbeth has a horrifying vision of a dagger dripping with blood before he goes to murder King Duncan.'
- An **analysis** is an explanation of the real meaning or significance that lies 'beneath' the text's words (and images, for a film). For example: 'Macbeth's vision of a bloody dagger shows how deeply uneasy he is about the violent act he is contemplating, and conveys his sense that supernatural forces are impelling him to act.'

A limited amount of summary is sometimes necessary to let your reader know which part of the text you wish to discuss. However, always keep this to a minimum and follow it immediately with your analysis of what this part of the text is really telling us.

Plan your essay

Carefully plan your essay so that you have a clear idea of what you are going to say. The plan ensures that your ideas flow logically, your argument remains consistent and you stay on topic. An essay plan should be a list **of brief dot points** covering no more than half a page.

- Include your central argument or main contention – a concise statement of your overall response to the topic.
- Write three or four dot points for each paragraph, indicating the main idea and evidence/examples from the text. In your essay you will need to *expand* on these points and *analyse* the evidence.

Structure your essay

An essay is a complete, self-contained piece of writing. It has a clear beginning (the introduction), middle (several body paragraphs) and end (the last paragraph or conclusion). It must also have a central argument that runs throughout, linking each paragraph to form a coherent whole. See examples of introductions and conclusions in the 'Analysing a sample topic' and 'Sample answer' sections.

The introduction establishes your overall response to the topic. It includes your main contention and outlines the main evidence you will refer to in the course of the essay. Write your introduction *after* you have done a plan and *before* you write the rest of the essay.

The body paragraphs argue your case – they present evidence from the text and explain how this evidence supports your argument. Each body paragraph needs:

- a strong **topic sentence** (usually the first sentence) that states the main point being made in the paragraph
- **evidence** from the text, including some brief quotations
- **analysis** of the textual evidence, with **explanation** of its significance and how it supports your argument
- **links back to the topic** in one or more statements, usually towards the end of the paragraph.

Connect the body paragraphs so that your discussion flows smoothly. Use some linking words and phrases such as 'similarly' and 'on the other hand', though don't start every paragraph like this. Another strategy is to use a significant word from the last sentence of one paragraph in the first sentence of the next.

Use key terms from the topic – or synonyms for them – throughout, so the relevance of your discussion to the topic is always clear.

The conclusion ties everything together and finishes the essay. It includes strong statements that emphasise your central argument and provide a clear response to the topic.

Avoid simply restating the points made earlier in the essay – this will end on a very flat note and imply that you have run out of ideas and vocabulary. The conclusion should be a logical extension of what you have written, not just a repetition or summary of it. Writing an effective conclusion can be a challenge. Try using these tips:

- Start by linking back to the final sentence of the second-last paragraph, rather than leaping to your main contention straight away – this helps your writing to flow.
- Use synonyms and expressions with equivalent meanings to vary your vocabulary. This allows you to reinforce your line of argument without being repetitive.
- When planning your essay, think of one or two broad statements or observations about the text's wider meaning. These should be related to the topic and your overall argument. Keep them for the conclusion, since they will give you something 'new' to say but still follow logically from your discussion. The introduction will be focused on the topic, but the conclusion can present a wider view of the text.

Essay topics

1 '*The Hunger Games* suggests that relationships are just as important in times of conflict as in times of peace.' Do you agree?

2 How does the first-person narration help to establish the theme of identity in *The Hunger Games*?

3 '*The Hunger Games* is a story about survival.' Discuss.

4 "Only I keep wishing I could think of a way to … to show the Capitol they don't own me. That I'm more than just a piece in their Games."
Discuss the importance of rebellion in *The Hunger Games*.

5 '*The Hunger Games* is a critique of modern-day mainstream culture.'
To what extent do you agree?

6 How do Katniss' experiences back home in District 12 help her to survive in the Hunger Games arena?

7 '*The Hunger Games* highlights the senselessness of death.' Discuss.

8 'In times of conflict, the characters in *The Hunger Games* demonstrate both the best and the worst of human behaviour.'
Discuss.

9 '"It's to the Capitol's advantage to have us divided among ourselves" he might say if there were no ears to hear but mine.'
How does *The Hunger Games* show the insidiousness of an oppressive government?

10 'Life for the characters in *The Hunger Games* is a constant struggle.'
Do you agree?

Analysing a sample topic

'*The Hunger Games* suggests that relationships are just as important in times of conflict as in times of peace.' Do you agree?

When analysing an essay topic, it is important to understand precisely *what* the topic is asking you to do. This means identifying key words and terms, as well as task words such as 'discuss' and 'explore'. In the case of the topic above, the type of question is 'Do you agree?'. This means that you will need to explore the topic from multiple angles but ultimately *resolve the tension* in the topic and answer the question.

This essay takes a fairly simple approach, focusing on Katniss and the relationships she has or develops with secondary characters. You could also discuss the relationships *between* these secondary characters.

Sample introduction

> Against a brutal and turbulent backdrop, relationships emerge as a central theme of Suzanne Collins' *The Hunger Games*. From the moment that Katniss volunteers as tribute and endangers her life, her survival is dependent on the connections she develops in the Capitol and in the arena, as well as those cultivated back home in District 12. While her intellect and skills are important to how she fares in the Games, Katniss is bolstered by the aid and moral support of others throughout her journey. The novel thus demonstrates how bonds of trust, solidarity and love can be instrumental in survival and resistance in times of conflict.

Body paragraph outline

Paragraph 1: The relationships that Katniss develops in the Capitol not only set her up for success in the arena but also help to protect her in its aftermath.

- Cinna becomes one of Katniss' closest friends and confidants. He is the last person she sees before entering the arena, and he supports her by sitting with her in silence and enclosing her hands 'in both of his' (p.177), providing her with the moral support she needs in that terrifying moment.
- Though they develop somewhat of a love-hate father-daughter relationship, Haymitch looks out for Katniss throughout the novel. In addition to providing her with supplies in her darkest moments in the arena, he also warns her that she's 'in trouble' (p.433) at the Games' conclusion and may face the wrath of the Capitol if she doesn't do as he says.

Paragraph 2: Building alliances based on trust is essential to Katniss' survival in the arena.

- Although the relationship between Katniss and Peeta is initially based on a strategic alliance to win the Games, it gradually evolves into genuine care, trust and even love.
- Katniss' close friendship with Rue, who reminds her of her younger sister, Prim, brings her joy in the arena. After Rue's death, Katniss is 'determined to avenge her, to make her loss unforgettable' (p.293), and this drives her through difficult moments in the arena.
- Thresh saves Katniss from Clove because of her alliance with and display of empathy to Rue, Thresh's fellow District 11 tribute.

Paragraph 3: Memories of happier times drive Katniss to overcome the obstacle of the Games and return to her former life.

- What keeps Katniss moving on and towards safety in particularly difficult moments is Prim, and the thought of her 'having to watch' (p.270) Katniss' death.
- Travelling through the woods of the arena, Katniss reflects on the days she spent hunting with Gale in the forest outside District 12: 'I just miss him' (p.136). This memory brings her joy and pushes her to return home safely.

Sample conclusion

> Through the character of Katniss, *The Hunger Games* presents a compelling argument for the importance of relationships in dire circumstances. Katniss initially believes that she can survive the threat of the Games by herself, but quickly learns that this will not be possible. Not only must she develop alliances against the other tributes, but she also requires human connections to help stave off loneliness and mental anguish. In addition, the thought of her loved ones back home pushes her to keep fighting, and ultimately win the Games. Even after her victory, her life remains in danger. Fortunately, she is guided to safety by individuals with whom she has developed a close bond, highlighting the continued importance of relationships in times of conflict.

SAMPLE ANSWER

'*The Hunger Games* is a critique of modern-day mainstream culture.' To what extent do you agree?

Although Suzanne Collins' *The Hunger Games* is set in a dystopian future, it nonetheless reflects and critiques several elements of modern-day society. Collins uses the fictional nation of Panem and its Capitol, which are situated in current-day North America, to address issues that we see in our own society, such as contemporary society's obsession with entertainment, social inequality and desensitisation to violence. These concepts are explored and critiqued through the story of Katniss Everdeen, a young girl who is thrust into a brutal televised battle for survival that was born from these negative elements of society. The way in which she is able to navigate these obstacles suggests that they can be challenged and overcome.

One of the most prominent themes of the book is its critique of modern entertainment culture. In the Capitol, the wealthy and powerful elite watch the Hunger Games as a form of entertainment, celebrating the violence and suffering of the tributes – as Katniss point out, 'they can't wait to watch us die'. The Games themselves are a grim spectacle, where children are forced to fight to the death for the amusement of the masses. More than that, they must partake in the rituals surrounding the Games, such as interviews in which they are required to present a version of themselves that will garner support and sponsors from the wealthy inhabitants of the Capitol. This engenders feelings of anger from competitors such as Katniss, who exclaims, 'Why am I hopping around like some trained dog trying to please people I hate?'. This bleak portrayal of a society that thrives on the suffering of others reflects the voyeuristic tendencies of modern mainstream culture. Reality television shows such as *Survivor* and *Big Brother*, which gained prominence in the early 2000s, share similarities with the Hunger Games, as they exploit personal conflicts and struggles for entertainment. These shows have achieved enormous popularity, highlighting society's fascination with watching others endure hardship and engage in cutthroat competitions. Collins' novel serves as a warning against the consequences of such an obsession, illustrating how it can lead to the dehumanisation of individuals.

Another vital aspect of the novel is its portrayal of socioeconomic inequality, a pressing issue in modern-day society. In the novel, the Capitol represents the privileged elite, while the twelve districts symbolise the marginalised and impoverished masses. The stark contrast between the opulent lifestyles of Capitol citizens and the abject poverty in the districts mirrors the growing income inequality in the real world. Katniss provides readers with examples of this disparity, noting that, unlike in the districts, 'food appears at the press of a button' in the Capitol and 'here there would be no shortage' of electricity. Today, income inequality is a global concern, with the rich becoming richer while the poor struggle to make ends meet. *The Hunger Games* echoes this disparity by depicting the Capitol's decadent excesses and the districts' desperate poverty. Katniss' struggle to provide for her family in District 12 resonates with individuals living in impoverished regions, underscoring the grim reality of the wealth gap.

Desensitisation to violence is another contemporary issue addressed by Collins. In the novel, the citizens of the Capitol view the violence of the Hunger Games as entertainment, desensitising them to the brutality and suffering it entails. When Katniss returns to the Capitol as a victor, her team of stylists barely register that she has been through a traumatic and violent experience; instead, 'everything is about them, not the dying boys and girls in the arena'. This parallels how modern society consumes violence through various media, from video games to graphic films, without fully comprehending its real-world consequences. The rise of violent video games, for instance, has sparked debates about their impact on individuals' empathy and perception of violence. *The Hunger Games* underscores the dangers of desensitisation, emphasising that when violence becomes a form of entertainment the consequences are dire. The novel challenges readers to reflect on their own consumption of violent media and its potential consequences for their empathy and moral values.

In conclusion, *The Hunger Games* by Suzanne Collins is undeniably a critique of modern-day mainstream culture. Through its portrayal of a society obsessed with entertainment, rampant socioeconomic inequality and desensitisation to violence, the novel highlights pressing issues that resonate with contemporary audiences. Collins' dystopian world serves as a warning, urging readers to reflect on the consequences of their actions and the values of the society they live in. Moreover, her novel challenges us to confront the darker aspects of modern society and encourages us to strive for a more just, empathetic and compassionate world. Through the lens of Katniss Everdeen's journey, we are reminded that the fight for a better society begins with acknowledging and addressing the flaws of our own culture.

REFERENCES & READING

Text

Collins, S 2008, *The Hunger Games*, Scholastic Press, New York.

References and further reading

Bradshaw, B 2012, *'The Hunger Games* – review', *The Guardian*, 22 March.

Collins, S, 'Biography', https://www.suzannecollinsbooks.com/bio.htm

Dominus, S 2011, 'Suzanne Collins's War Stories for Kids', *The New York Times*, 8 April.

Grady, C, St James, E, Barkhorn, E, Abad-Santos, A & Romano, A 2018, '10 years later, is *The Hunger Games* still shocking?', Vox, 19 December.

Green, J 2008, 'Scary New World', *The New York Times*, 7 November.

Hughes, S 2015, 'In debt, out of luck: why Generation K fell in love with *The Hunger Games*', *The Guardian*, 31 October.

King, S 2008, *'The Hunger Games'*, *Entertainment Weekly*, 8 September.

Lambert, I 2022, 'Looking Back on *The Hunger Games*: 10 Years Later', *Video Librarian*, 23 March.

The New York Times 2018, 'Suzanne Collins Talks About *The Hunger Games*, the Books and the Movies', 18 October.